Training Manual
for
What Every Teacher
Should Know

WHAT EVERY TEACHER SHOULD KNOW

The 10-Book Collection by Donna Walker Tileston

DONNA WALKER TILESTON

Training Manual
for
What Every Teacher Should Know

CORWIN PRESS
A Sage Publications Company
Thousand Oaks, California

For information:

Corwin Press
A Sage Publications Company
2455 Teller Road
Thousand Oaks, California 91320
E-mail: order@corwinpress.com

Sage Publications Ltd.
1 Oliver's Yard
55 City Road
London EC1Y 1SP
United Kingdom

Sage Publications India Pvt. Ltd.
B-42, Panchsheel Enclave
Post Box 4109
New Delhi 110 017 India

Printed in the United States of America

Library of Congress Cataloging-in-Publication Data

Tileston, Donna Walker.
Training manual for what every teacher should know / Donna Walker Tileston.
    p. cm.
Includes bibliographical references.
ISBN 0-7619-3999-7 (pbk.)
  1. Teachers—In-service training—Handbooks, manuals, etc. 2. Teaching.
I. Tileston, Donna Walker. What every teacher should know about—II. Title.
LB1731.T54 2005
370'.71'55—dc22

                        2004018163

This book is printed on acid-free paper.

05   06   07   08   09   10 9 8 7 6 5 4 3 2 1

Acquisitions Editor:	Faye Zucker
Editorial Assistants:	Stacy Wagner/Gem Rabanera
Production Editor:	Tracy Alpern
Copy Editor:	Stacey Shimizu
Proofreader:	Kevin Gleason
Typesetter:	C&M Digitals (P) Ltd.
Cover Designer:	Tracy E. Miller
Graphic Designer:	Lisa Miller

Contents

Preface

The series *What Every Teacher Should Know* was written to help educators navigate the complex maze of teaching. It gives practical information about important classroom topics and helps teachers refine their skills to become dynamic, engaging, life-long educators.

How many workshops tell educators that they need to be doing something—yet do not teach them how to do it? *What Every Teacher Should Know* gives practical information and strategies teachers need to make students more successful, while the activities in this training manual provide an opportunity for teachers to implement what they have learned. Reading the books provides participants with valuable information, but meaningful dialogue with other professionals deepens their understanding. The training manual is designed to help professional development facilitators guide the participants through numerous exercises and activities to gain maximum benefit from the research and theory provided in the text.

Professional development must be more than "sit and get" sessions. It must be a high-quality training program that is relevant to day-to-day teaching, aligns with the school goals, and includes follow-up and support (National Staff Development Council, 2001). Professionals need sufficient time and support to construct meaning and to translate what they are learning into daily practice. The time and support necessary for valuable, high-quality professional development are built into this book series and training program. Throughout this training, professionals will engage in meaningful, purposeful dialogue concerning differentiation in the use of time, planning, and instructional practices to meet the needs of all learners.

ACKNOWLEDGMENTS

Many thanks to Dr. Jeannie Grishem and Ronnie Porter for their creative talents to this work.

And thank you to Faye Zucker and the team at Corwin Press for their belief in me and my work.

About the Author

Donna Walker Tileston, Ed.D., is a veteran teacher of three decades and the president of Strategic Teaching and Learning, a consulting firm that provides services to schools throughout the United States and Canada. Her publications include *Strategies for Teaching Differently: On the Block or Not* (1998), *Innovative Strategies of the Block Schedule* (1999), and *Ten Best Teaching Practices: How Brain Research, Learning Styles, and Standards Define Teaching Competencies* (2000), which has been on Corwin's best-seller list since its first year in print.

She received her bachelor's degree from the University of North Texas, her master's from East Texas State University, and her doctorate from Texas A & M University Commerce. She currently is with Strategic Teaching & Learning in Dallas, Texas, www.strategicteachinglearning.com.

Her 10-book *What Every Teacher Should Know* collection received the Association of Educational Publishers' 2004 Distinguished Achievement Award for Excellence in Educational Publishing as a handbook for professional development for adults. This training manual is based on that award-winning collection.

Introduction for the Facilitator

Professional development programs are necessary to increase student achievement. Effective professional development programs utilize research-based practices. The *What Every Teacher Should Know* series is based on current research literature. This training manual is designed to provide adult learners with the theory behind effective practices, a model of effective practices, initial practice during the sessions, classroom connection exercises, and prompt feedback from the training facilitator.

Each chapter in this training manual connects to one book in the series. The training chapters are designed to focus on one book at a time; however, the material and time frames are flexible. You may consider a one-day workshop for the entire chapter or two half-day sessions, or you may want to divide the activities into a series of short sessions (for example, weekly meetings).

The climate of the session is crucial for success. Teachers are professionals, so you should consider the following:

- *The Time for the Training.* Teachers need uninterrupted time to engage in meaningful dialogue. Set the training schedule far enough in advance so that teachers can prepare and understand the importance of the workshop.
- *The Room Arrangement.* Arrange the furniture so the room feels open and comfortable. Place the tables or desks in a manner conducive to cooperative learning groups. Make sure everyone can easily see the facilitator.
- *The Agenda.* Post an agenda or daily training schedule for each session. Teachers benefit from knowing what is occurring and when is it occurring.
- *Refreshments.* It is important to provide food and drinks for the session.
- *Using Music.* Play appropriate music to begin the workshop, during transitions, or to energize the group when necessary. According to Allen (2001), "Music is an incredibly powerful instructional tool which can be added to most, if not all, learning situations. It has a direct physical, emotional, and psychological effect . . ." (p. 33).
- *The Rules and Norms for the Group.* You can make the training very successful by providing ground rules or norms for the group. Participants need to know what is expected and what to expect. If possible, involve the participants in establishing the rules and norms. Following is a suggested list of ground rules:

    Be on time.

    Stay on schedule.

    One person speaks at a time.

Actively participate.

If you think it, say it.

What is said here, stays here; what is learned here, leaves here.

Take care of your needs.

Have fun!

BEFORE THE TRAINING

As you prepare for the workshop, there are several tasks you will need to complete. First, procure a set of *What Every Teacher Should Know: The 10-Book Collection* for each participant (or the appropriate title for the session) and distribute them prior to the workshop. Assign the reading to be completed for the session(s). If you are implementing a one-day workshop, ask participants to read the desired book before the session. If, however, you are teaching the book in multiple sessions, assign the appropriate chapters or sections of the desired book. Second, review the material in the book and in this training manual.

Prepare an agenda for the session and distribute to all participants. Next, secure an appropriate location and schedule adequate time for the workshop. Inform the participants of the time, place, purpose, required materials, and required reading for the meeting. It is helpful to send participants a reminder a few days prior to the meeting.

Finally, set up the room in a manner conducive to dialogue and cooperative learning groups. Have furniture, technological devices, and materials accessible and in working order. Organize refreshments for the session and place them in a convenient location.

Materials

You will need the following materials for the workshops:

A set of *What Every Teacher Should Know: The 10-Book Collection* for each participant (or the appropriate volume in the set)

Handouts for each participant

Transparencies of all reproducibles and an overhead projector (or other form of digital presentation)

Pens, pencils, markers, and highlighters

Chart paper

Tape, staples, pushpins, clips, or easels to display chart paper

Notepads or reusable notepaper

Note cards

A copy of state academic standards

A CD player and music (recommended)

Throughout the training, there are some general reproducibles that you will want to reference repeatedly (see Reproducible 0.1, Cooperative Learning Group Roles and Guidelines, and Reproducible 0.2, Rules for Brainstorming). Consider creating transparencies and storing them in clear sheet protectors; or consider using a digital presentation.

Make a copy of the Facilitator Evaluation Survey (Reproducible 0.3) for each participant. At the conclusion of the session, ask participants to give you feedback about the workshop. Use their responses to reflect on your own performance and how to improve the professional development experience.

Learning Objectives

Each chapter includes declarative and procedural objectives for the activities. Declarative objectives are based on factual information that the participants will know as a result of the training. Procedural objectives refer to what the participants will be able to do as a result of the training. Why is it important to differentiate between the two? We should teach declarative information differently than we do procedural information so that both are stored appropriately in the brain for recall. Declarative information needs a "connector" so that it is stored more effectively. It is important to share the objectives before conducting the activity. You will find the objectives listed at the beginning of each chapter and identified for each activity.

Reproducible 0.1. Cooperative Learning Group Roles and Guidelines

Pilot: Keeps the group running smoothly. Ensures that all tasks are completed.

Recorder: Writes down the thoughts/solutions as directed by the group.

Reporter: Gives progress report when the group is ready to share with the leader or large group.

Materials Keeper: Retrieves and returns materials as needed.

Encourager: Praises group members for work. Leads cheers.

Timekeeper: Ensures that all work is completed on time.

Guidelines for Collaborative Work

- Work together in groups of three to five.
- Share leadership of the group.
- Assign a role for each member of the group. Individuals may need to fulfill more than one role.
- Listen carefully to others and build upon their ideas.
- Ensure that all participate and no one dominates.
- Proceed at a pace that is comfortable for the group.
- Cooperate with other group members.
- Achieve a group solution and be mindful of time restraints.
- Ensure that all group members understand the solution before moving on.

Reproducible 0.2. Rules for Brainstorming

- Get as many ideas on the table as possible.
- Accept all ideas without judgment.
- Stretch for new ideas.
- Edit, combine, or connect ideas only after the brainstorm is finished.

Reproducible 0.3. Facilitator Evaluation Survey

Directions: Please complete the following survey by circling the answer choice after each statement that best represents your view.

1 = Strongly Agree   2 = Agree   3 = Disagree   4 = Strongly Disagree

1. The goals and objectives of the workshop were clearly articulated.   1   2   3   4

2. The facilitator presented all information necessary for completing each activity.   1   2   3   4

3. The facilitator presented all information in a way that facilitated productive participation.   1   2   3   4

4. The information presented was relevant to my daily classroom responsibilities.   1   2   3   4

5. I can implement what I have learned in my classroom.   1   2   3   4

6. The activities were structured to maximize learning.   1   2   3   4

7. My participation was important to the success of my learning group.   1   2   3   4

8. The visuals and handouts increased awareness and understanding.   1   2   3   4

9. The learning environment was conducive to learning.   1   2   3   4

10. I would recommend this workshop to others.   1   2   3   4

Comments:

_____

_____

_____

_____

Training Session 1

What Every Teacher Should Know About Diverse Learners

Today's learners are different in many ways, such as race, ethnicity, socioeconomic status, gender, learning modalities, cognitive development, social development, and the rate at which they take in and retrieve information. In other words, today's learners are diverse. The book *What Every Teacher Should Know About Diverse Learners* examines the characteristics of student diversity, bias, closing the achievement gap, and strategies to use with a diverse student population. Each student in the classroom is unique. The successful teacher recognizes how student diversity affects learning and creates a classroom in which diversity is celebrated and revered.

MATERIALS

You will need the following materials for this session:

A copy of *What Every Teacher Should Know About Diverse Learners* for each participant

Handouts for each participant

Transparencies of all reproducibles and an overhead projector (or other form of digital presentation)

Pens, pencils, markers, and highlighters

Chart paper

Tape, staples, pushpins, clips, or easels to display chart paper

Notepads or reusable notepaper

A CD player and music (recommended)

LEARNING OBJECTIVES

Declarative Objectives

Participants will know the following:

- What diverse learners are and how they affect schools
- The terminology related to diverse learners
- Their personal beliefs concerning learning styles, socioeconomic status, and culture
- The author's beliefs concerning learning styles, socioeconomic status, and culture
- The six types of bias: Isolation, Selectivity, Unreality, Linguistic Bias, Exclusion, and Stereotyping
- The strategies that positively affect diverse learners

Procedural Objectives

Participants will be able to do the following:

- Create a Thought Wheel that details their knowledge of diverse learners
- Define the terminology related to diverse learners
- Assess their knowledge about diverse learners
- List their personal beliefs concerning learning styles, socioeconomic status, and culture
- List the author's beliefs concerning learning styles, socioeconomic status, and culture
- Construct conclusions concerning their beliefs regarding learning styles, socioeconomic status, and culture
- Classify the six types of bias: Isolation, Selectivity, Unreality, Linguistic Bias, Exclusion, and Stereotyping
- Describe the strategies that positively affect diverse learners
- Implement two or three of the diverse strategies described
- Reflect on their knowledge about diverse learners

Suggested Activities and Time Frame

Estimated Time: 6 hours

Estimated Time on Task	Objectives	Activities
20 minutes	Declarative Objective—Participants will know • What diverse learners are and how they affect schools. Procedural Objective—Participants will be able to • Create a Thought Wheel that details their knowledge of diverse learners.	**Activity 1: Preparing for the Learning** Invite the participants to form cooperative learning groups. Refer to Reproducible 0.1. Tell the participants that they will engage in a brainstorming activity to access prior knowledge. Share the rules of brainstorming on Reproducible 0.2. Display and model how to create a Thought Wheel using Reproducible 1.1. Give each group a sheet of chart paper and ask the recorders to create a Thought Wheel on the paper. Instruct the recorders to write *Diverse Learners* in the center circle. Prompt the groups to brainstorm all that they know about diverse learners and have the recorders jot down words and phrases in the second tier of the Thought Wheel. Finally, ask participants to brainstorm the impacts of diverse learners on schools and record the ideas on the outer circle of the Thought Wheel. Invite the reporters to share their Thought Wheels with the large group. Introduce the topic of the workshop—*What Every Teacher Should Know About Diverse Learners.* Share the declarative and procedural objectives for the training. Refer the participants to the book *What Every Teacher Should Know About Diverse Learners.* Tell them that the activities in this workshop are designed to engage the participants in meaningful dialogue concerning diverse learners.
45 minutes	Declarative Objective—Participants will know • The terminology related to diverse learners.	**Activity 2: Examining the Vocabulary** Review and post the objectives for the activity. Remind the participants of the roles and guidelines of their cooperative learning groups (see Reproducible 0.1).

(Continued)

(Continued)

Estimated Time on Task	Objectives	Activities
	Procedural Objective—Participants will be able to • Define the terminology related to diverse learners.	Refer participants to the Vocabulary List for Assessment in *What Every Teacher Should Know About Diverse Learners* (p. xiii). Instruct participants to provide a definition for each vocabulary word based on what they already know. Have them write their definitions in the column "Your Definition." Divide the vocabulary words equally among the groups. Ask the groups to discuss their assigned words, check the Vocabulary Summary, and review the text of the book to refine their definitions. Have them write the new definitions in the column "Your Revised Definition." Invite the reporters to share their revised definitions with the large group.
15 minutes	Procedural Objective—Participants will be able to • Assess their knowledge about diverse learners.	**Pre-Test** Review and post the objective for the activity. Inform the group that it is important to assess the knowledge they bring to the workshop. At the conclusion of the workshop, they will be able to measure their learning and progress. Refer participants to the Vocabulary Pre-Test section of the book *What Every Teacher Should Know About Diverse Learners* (beginning on p. xv). Have participants complete the test, and then direct them to the Post-Test Answer Key in the book *What Every Teacher Should Know About Diverse Learners* (p. 82). Ask participants to grade their tests and record the number of correct answers for future reference.
30–45 minutes	Declarative Objectives—Participants will know • Their personal beliefs concerning learning styles, socioeconomic status, and culture.	**Activity 3: Making Use of the Information From the Book** *Part I—Examining Differences* Review and post the objectives for the activity.

Estimated Time on Task	Objectives	Activities
	• The author's beliefs concerning learning styles, socioeconomic status, and culture.	Refer participants to Chapter 2 of the book *What Every Teacher Should Know About Diverse Learners.* Before reading, have participants complete the first half of the activity.
	Procedural Objectives— Participants will be able to	Make a copy of the A Closer Look at Me worksheet (Reproducible 1.2) for each participant. Before reading the chapter, direct participants to write down their beliefs and attitudes about diverse learning in schools.
	• List their personal beliefs concerning learning styles, socioeconomic status, and culture.	Once participants have read the chapter, tell them to complete Boxes 4–6 on the reproducible.
	• List the author's beliefs concerning learning styles, socioeconomic status, and culture.	Monitor the participants during the activity; provide assistance and answer questions as needed. After everyone has completed the worksheet, invite volunteers to share their thoughts and insights. Record new knowledge on chart paper for everyone to see.
	• Construct conclusions concerning their beliefs regarding learning styles, socioeconomic status, and culture.	
30–45 minutes	Declarative Objective— Participants will know	**Activity 3: Making Use of the Information From the Book**
	• The six types of bias: Isolation, Selectivity, Unreality, Linguistic Bias, Exclusion, and Stereotyping.	*Part II—Recognizing Bias*

Review and post the objectives for the activity.

Remind the participants of the roles and guidelines for cooperative learning groups (see Reproducible 0.1). |
| | Procedural Objective— Participants will be able to | Remind participants about what they read in Chapter 3 of the book *What Every Teacher Should Know About Diverse Learners.* |
| | • Classify the six types of bias: Isolation, Selectivity, Unreality, Linguistic Bias, Exclusion, and Stereotyping. | Review and model how to complete the Bias Tree found on Reproducible 1.3.

Give each group a sheet of chart paper. Prompt the recorders to recreate the Bias Tree on the paper. Encourage the groups to discuss what they learned about bias and record the details and examples on the tree. |

(Continued)

(Continued)

Estimated Time on Task	*Objectives*	*Activities*
		When all groups are finished, ask the reporters to post the Bias Trees around the room. Invite participants to review the work of all groups.
35 minutes	Procedural Objective—Participants will be able to • Assess their knowledge about diverse learners.	**Activity 4: Knowledge and Confidence** Review and post the objective for the activity. Tell the participants that they have reviewed the vocabulary, read the book, and actively discussed the topic of diverse learners. Ask them to assess their knowledge and confidence in applying the information they have learned. Make a copy of the Diverse Learners Survey (Reproducible 1.4) for each participant. Have them complete the survey individually. Then, in their learning groups, encourage participants to discuss the results and create a chart of new knowledge and insights. Invite the reporters to share the lists with the large group.
50 minutes	Declarative Objective—Participants will know • How to implement strategies that positively affect diverse learners. Procedural Objectives—Participants will be able to • Describe the strategies that positively affect diverse learners. • Implement two or three of the diverse strategies they described.	**Activity 5: Practical Application in the Classroom** Review and post the objectives for the activity. Refer participants to Chapters 4–6 of the book *What Every Teacher Should Know About Diverse Learners.* Explain to them that they will investigate various strategies to use in their own classrooms to help meet the needs of diverse learners. Give each participant a copy of the Closing the Gap handout (Reproducible 1.5). Have them describe five strategies they learned about that they are willing to implement tomorrow in their own classrooms. After they have completed the form, direct participants to use two or three of the strategies when they return to their classrooms.

Estimated Time on Task	Objectives	Activities
		Encourage participants to record their progress by keeping a journal, collecting evidence, or videotaping their classrooms. During subsequent sessions, invite participants to share their successes and request more guidance.
45 minutes	Procedural Objective—Participants will be able to • Assess their knowledge about diverse learners.	**Activity 6: Self-Evaluation** Review and post the objective for the activity. Ask participants to join their cooperative groups. Direct them to talk about their successes with implementing the new strategies (as described in the previous activity) in their classrooms. Have the reporters share one or two anecdotes from the discussion with the large group. Prompt participants to complete the Vocabulary Post-Test beginning on page 77 of the book *What Every Teacher Should Know About Diverse Learners*. Have participants grade their Post-Tests and record the number of correct responses. Then, ask them to compare results to the Pre-Test.
15 minutes	Procedural Objective—Participants will be able to • Reflect on their knowledge about diverse learners.	**Activity 7: Reflection** Review and post the objective for the activity. Refer to the Boy and the Bubble worksheet (Reproducible 1.6). Ask each participant to write in the thought bubble the most important thing they learned about diverse learners during this workshop. When participants are finished, invite volunteers to share their thoughts about their learning. If appropriate, have the participants complete the Facilitator Evaluation Survey (Reproducible 0.3) for the training.

Reproducible 1.1. Thought Wheel Brainstorming Activity

Directions: In the center circle, write *Diverse Learners.* In the second tier, brainstorm words and phrases about diverse learners. In the outside circle, write about the impact diverse learners have on schools.

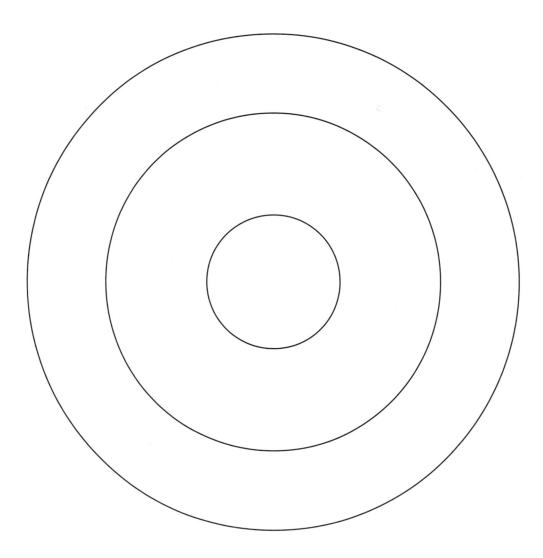

Reproducible 1.2. A Closer Look at Me: A Tool for Identifying Personal Bias

In Boxes 1–3, list your beliefs and attitudes prior to reading Chapter 2, "How Are We Diverse"

After reading Chapter 2, explain the author's beliefs about each topic in boxes 4–6.

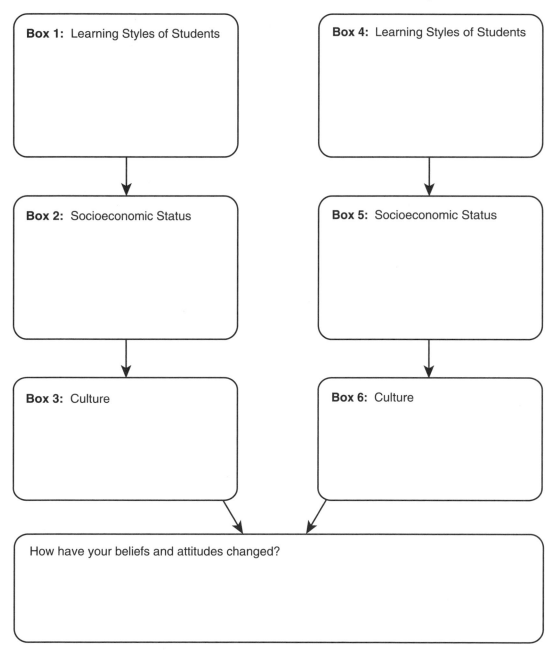

Box 1: Learning Styles of Students

Box 2: Socioeconomic Status

Box 3: Culture

Box 4: Learning Styles of Students

Box 5: Socioeconomic Status

Box 6: Culture

How have your beliefs and attitudes changed?

Reproducible 1.3. The Bias Tree:
A Tool for Classifying the Types of Bias

Directions: Read the chapter "Recognizing the Signs of Bias" in the book *What Every Teacher Should Know About Diverse Learners*. On the tree, list details and examples for each type of bias.

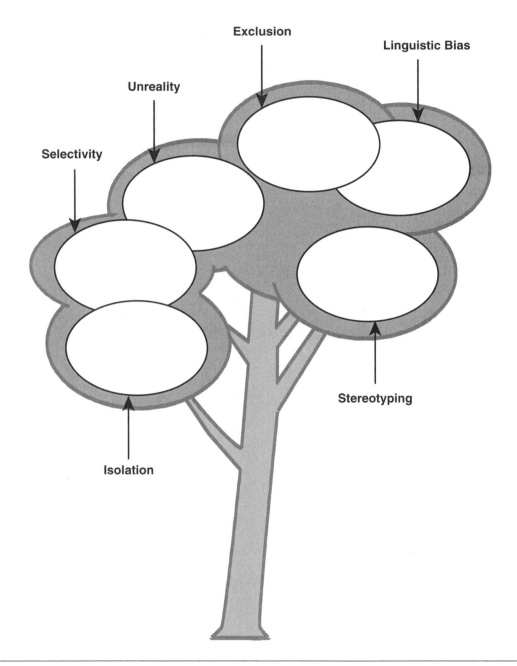

Reproducible 1.4. Diverse Learners Survey: A Tool to Help Educators Determine Their Level of Understanding

Directions: For each topic, place an X in the Knowledge column that demonstrates your level of understanding. Next, rate your Confidence Level regarding each statement.

Examining Diversity	*Knowledge*	
A. I understand the impact and importance of diversity on student achievement.	Yes	No

How confident are you? Rate your level of confidence.	Rating Scale (Place a check mark in the appropriate column)			
	Not Confident			Very Confident
	1	**2**	**3**	**4**
1. I understand the importance of the impact of the classroom teacher on climate.				
2. I have examined my attitudes related to diversity.				
3. I understand how to analyze instructional materials to ensure proper reflection of student populations.				
4. I implement strategies that meet the learning styles and needs of the students in my classroom.				
5. I implement effective instructional techniques that meet the needs of students from poverty.				
6. I understand the type of learning style to utilize when reteaching students in the classroom.				
7. I implement strategies to identify the preferred learning styles of my students.				
8. I understand the importance of varying activities to meet the needs of a diverse student population.				
9. I understand the characteristics and needs of the differing socioeconomic groups in my classroom.				
10. I understand the research-based strategies that have the greatest impact on learning for my diverse student population.				

(Continued)

(Continued)

Recognizing Bias	Knowledge	
B. I understand the impact of bias on the teaching/ learning process.	Yes	No

How confident are you? Rate your level of confidence.	Rating Scale (Place a check mark in the appropriate column) Not Confident Very Confident			
	1	**2**	**3**	**4**
11. I understand the impact of linguistic bias on the teaching/learning process and how to avoid it.				
12. I understand the impact of stereotyping on the teaching/ learning process and how to avoid it.				
13. I understand the impact of exclusion on the teaching/learning process and how to avoid it.				
14. I understand the impact of unreality on the teaching/learning process and how to avoid it.				
15. I understand the impact of selectivity on the teaching/learning process and how to avoid it.				
16. I understand the impact of isolation on the teaching/learning process.				

Closing the Achievement Gap	*Knowledge*	
C. I understand how to implement strategies that have a positive impact on achievement for all students.	Yes	No

How confident are you? Rate your level of confidence.	Rating Scale (Place a check mark in the appropriate column) Not Confident Very Confident			
	1	**2**	**3**	**4**
17. I incorporate strategies that promote relationship building.				
18. I implement strategies to build resiliency in my students.				
19. I provide accurate information about cultural groups through straightforward discussions of race, ethnicity, and other cultural differences.				
20. I implement strategies to access the self-system of the brain.				
21. I understand how to implement strategies to access prior knowledge.				
22. I implement strategies to meet the needs of second-language learners.				
23. I implement strategies that will help students to be successful at school and away from school.				
24. I implement strategies that assist students in setting learning goals.				
25. I implement strategies that demonstrate my understanding of the power of the brain in learning.				

Reproducible 1.5. Closing the Gap:
A Guide for Developing Personal Strategies

Directions: Describe five strategies that you can implement immediately to meet the needs of diverse learners in your classroom.

Reproducible 1.6. The Boy and the Bubble: Reflecting on the Learning

Directions: In the thought bubble, describe the most important thing you learned during this workshop.

Training Session 2

What Every Teacher Should Know About Student Motivation

What a wonderful time to be a teacher! Never before have we had before us the answers to unlock the mysteries of the mind or to change the world in the way that we have at this time. Through brain research and its implications for learning and remembering, we truly have the tools to work smarter. Never before have we had the opportunity to make positive change in today's troubled classrooms that we have today.

Thanks to the work of people like Marzano (1992, 1998, 2001) and Jensen (1997, 1998), we know that learning does not begin with the cognitive system of the brain. Rather, learning begins in the self-system of the brain, and it is this system that decides whether the learning is worthy of our attention. *What Every Teacher Should Know About Student Motivation* provides a strategic guide to help you activate motivation in your students.

MATERIALS

You will need the following materials for this session:

A copy of *What Every Teacher Should Know About Student Motivation* for each participant

Handouts for each participant

Transparencies of all reproducibles and an overhead projector (or other form of digital presentation)

Pens, pencils, markers, and highlighters

Chart paper

Tape, staples, pushpins, clips, or easels to display chart paper

Notepads or reusable notepaper

A CD player and music (recommended)

LEARNING OBJECTIVES

Declarative Objectives

Participants will know the following:

- How to define and explain student motivation
- The terminology related to student motivation
- The characteristics of rewards and celebrations; intrinsic and extrinsic motivation; the self-system and the metacognitive system; and self-efficacy and self-esteem
- How motivation relates to the beginning of a task
- How to encourage students to complete tasks
- The strategies to implement to ensure student motivation
- The components of the Model for Changing Demotivation to Motivation

Procedural Objectives

Participants will be able to do the following:

- Create a Mind Map that details their knowledge of student motivation
- Define the terminology related to student motivation
- Assess their knowledge about student motivation
- Compare and contrast the characteristics of rewards and celebrations; intrinsic and extrinsic motivation; the self-system and the metacognitive system; and self-efficacy and self-esteem
- List key learning points concerning motivation and beginning tasks
- Form conclusions concerning motivation and beginning tasks
- List ways to encourage students to complete tasks
- Form conclusions concerning ways to encourage students to complete tasks
- Design a model for changing unmotivated to motivated students

Suggested Activities and Time Frame

Estimated Time: 6 hours

Estimated Time on Task	Objectives	Activities
20 minutes	Declarative Objective— Participants will know • How to define and explain student motivation. Procedural Objective— Participants will • Create a Mind Map that details their knowledge of student motivation.	**Activity 1: Preparing for the Learning** Invite the participants to form cooperative learning groups. Refer to Reproducible 0.1. Tell the participants that they will engage in a brainstorming activity to access prior knowledge. Share the rules of brainstorming on Reproducible 0.2. Explain and model how to create a Mind Map using Reproducible 2.1. Give each group a sheet of chart paper. Ask the recorders to recreate the Mind Map on the paper. Instruct the groups to create a Mind Map about everything they already know about student motivation. When all groups have finished, invite the reporters to post the charts around the room and share their insights with the large group. Introduce the topic of the workshop—*What Every Teacher Should Know About Student Motivation.* Share the declarative and procedural objectives for the training. Refer the participants to the book *What Every Teacher Should Know About Student Motivation.* Tell them that the activities in this workshop are designed to engage the participants in meaningful dialogue concerning student motivation.
45 minutes	Declarative Objective— Participants will know: • The terminology related to student motivation. Procedural Objective— Participants will: • Define the terminology related to student motivation.	**Activity 2: Examining the Vocabulary** Review and post the objectives for the activity. Remind the participants of the roles and guidelines for cooperative learning groups (see Reproducible 0.1). Refer participants to the Vocabulary List for Assessment in *What Every Teacher Should Know About Student Motivation* (p. xiii).

(Continued)

(Continued)

Estimated Time on Task	*Objectives*	*Activities*
		Instruct participants to provide a definition for each vocabulary word based on what they already know. Have them write their definitions in the column "Your Definition."
		Divide the vocabulary words equally among the groups. Ask the groups to discuss their assigned words, check the Vocabulary Summary, and review the text of the book to refine their definitions. Have them write the new definitions in the column "Your Revised Definition."
		Invite the reporters to share their revised definitions with the large group.
15 minutes	Procedural Objective—Participants will be able to • Assess their knowledge about student motivation.	**Pre-Test** Review and post the objective for the activity. Inform the group that it is important to assess the knowledge they bring to the workshop. At the conclusion of the workshop, they will be able to measure their learning and progress. Refer participants to the Vocabulary Pre-Test section of the book *What Every Teacher Should Know About Student Motivation* (beginning on p. xv). Have participants complete the test, and then direct them to the Post-Test Answer Key in the book *What Every Teacher Should Know About Student Motivation* (p. 76). Ask participants to grade their tests and record the number of correct answers for future reference.
30–45 minutes	Declarative Objective—Participants will know: • The characteristics of rewards and celebrations; intrinsic and extrinsic motivation; the self-system and the metacognitive system; and self-efficacy and self-esteem.	**Activity 3: Making Use of the Information From the Book** *Part I—Students and Motivation* Review and post the objectives for the activity. Remind the participants of the roles and guidelines for cooperative learning groups (see Reproducible 0.1). Refer the participants to Chapters 1 and 2 in the book *What Every Teacher Should Know About Student Motivation.*

Estimated Time on Task	Objectives	Activities
	Procedural Objective— Participants will be able to: • Compare and contrast the characteristics of rewards and celebrations; intrinsic and extrinsic motivation; the self-system and the metacognitive system; and self-efficacy and self-esteem.	Review and model how to complete the Similarities/Differences Organizer using Reproducible 2.2. Give each group a copy of the Similarities/ Differences Organizer (Reproducible 2.2). You can give them each a transparency if you want them to display it on the overhead projector while sharing. Assign each group one set of the following topics: Rewards/Celebration; Intrinsic/Extrinsic Motivation; Self-System/Metacognitive System; Self-Efficacy/Self-Esteem. Have the groups compare and contrast the two ideas using information from the book. Each recorder is to complete one Similarities/Differences Organizer for the group. At the top of the organizer, have them list the two topics. Next, in the box provided, have them state the similarities. Finally, have them write the differences in the corresponding boxes. When the groups are finished, invite the reporters to present their findings to the large group. Have them report orally or display a transparency on an overhead projector.
30–45 minutes	Declarative Objectives— Participants will know • How motivation relates to the beginning of a task. • How to encourage students to complete tasks. Procedural Objectives— Participants will be able to • List key learning points concerning motivation and beginning tasks. • Form conclusions concerning motivation and beginning tasks.	**Activity 3: Making Use of the Information From the Book** *Part II—Understanding and Using the Elements of Student Motivation to Improve Instruction* Review and post the objectives for the activity. Refer participants to Chapters 3 and 4 in the book *What Every Teacher Should Know About Student Motivation.* Note: Participants will not form their usual cooperative groups. Have all participants form a large circle around the room. Ask them to number off from 1 to 4, so that you have four groups with approximately the same number of people. Direct all the 1s to one corner of the room, the 2s to another corner of the room, and so on. The four groups should be in opposing corners of the room.

(Continued)

(Continued)

Estimated Time on Task	Objectives	Activities
	• List ways to encourage students to complete tasks. • Form conclusions concerning ways to encourage students to complete tasks.	Tell each group what their topics will be: *Group 1:* Getting the Brain's Attention; What Is the Role of Self-Attributes?; What Is the Role of the Self and Others?; What Is the Role of the Students' Perception of the Nature of the World? *Group 2:* How Does Climate Affect Motivation? How Is Importance Related to Motivation? Why Is Efficacy Important to Motivation? *Group 3:* Activating the Metacognitive System *Group 4:* What About Minor Off-Task Behavior? Within their groups, prompt participants to review the book *What Every Teacher Should Know About Student Motivation* and discuss what they have learned about the assigned topic. Make a copy of the Four Corners Information Chart (Reproducible 2.3) for each group. Instruct someone to recreate the chart onto chart paper. After the groups hold their discussions, tell the recorder to write down the Three Key Learning Points and the Significant Implications in the appropriate places on the chart. Finally, have the groups post their charts on a wall in their respective corners. Show participants how to move, as a group, to each corner of the room. (You may want to play music while people are moving about the room.) At each corner, encourage participants to reflect on the key points and significant implications of the other topics. When everyone has had a chance to review all four corners, host a large group discussion to debrief the results.
35 minutes	Procedural Objective—Participants will be able to • Assess their knowledge about student motivation.	**Activity 4: Knowledge and Confidence** Review and post the objective for the activity. Tell the participants that they have reviewed the vocabulary, read the book, and actively discussed the topic of student motivation. Ask them to assess their knowledge and confidence in applying the information they have learned.

Estimated Time on Task	Objectives	Activities
		Make a copy of the Student Motivation Survey (Reproducible 2.4) for each participant. Have them complete the survey individually. Then, in their learning groups, encourage participants to discuss the results and create a chart of new knowledge and insights. Invite the reporters to share the lists with the large group.
20 minutes	Declarative Objectives— Participants will know • The strategies to implement to ensure student motivation. • The components of the Model for Changing Demotivation to Motivation. Procedural Objective— Participants will be able to • Design a model for changing unmotivated to motivated students.	**Activity 5: Practical Application in the Classroom** Review and post the objectives for the activity. Tell the participants that they will design a model for helping unmotivated students become motivated in the classroom. Have participants review Chapters 5 and 6 of the book *What Every Teacher Should Know About Student Motivation.* Display a copy of Reproducible 2.5. Explain and model how to complete the activity. Give participants a copy of Model for Changing Demotivation to Motivation (Reproducible 2.5) and instruct them to create their own model for motivating students in their classrooms. Encourage participants to refer back to Shanna Walker's model in Chapter 5 of *What Every Teacher Should Know About Student Motivation.* Note: If the workshop is being conducted in multiple sessions, you can ask the participants to complete the model at their discretion and use the strategies in their own classrooms. Encourage participants to record their progress with the implementation by keeping a journal, collecting evidence, or videotaping their classrooms. During subsequent sessions, invite participants to share their success and request more guidance. If the workshop is conducted in a one- or two-day session, have participants complete the model during the session and share their ideas within their groups. However, the classroom model should be developed by each participant individually.

(Continued)

(Continued)

Estimated Time on Task	Objectives	Activities
45 minutes	Procedural Objective—Participants will be able to • Assess their knowledge about student motivation.	**Activity 6: Self-Evaluation** Review and post the objective for the activity. Direct participants to share their motivation models (from Activity 5) within their learning groups. Prompt participants to complete the Vocabulary Post-Test beginning on page 71 in the book *What Every Teacher Should Know About Student Motivation.* Have participants grade their Post-Tests and record the number of correct responses. Then, ask them to compare the results to the Pre-Test.
45 minutes	Procedural Objective—Participants will be able to • Assess their knowledge about student motivation.	**Activity 7: Reflection** Review and post the objective for the activity. Review the Three W's Chart (Reproducible 2.6) with participants. Ask them to complete the Three W's Chart on their own, and then discuss individual responses within their cooperative groups. Ask the reporters to share any new insights with the large group. If appropriate, have the participants complete the Facilitator Evaluation Survey (Reproducible 0.3) for the training.

Reproducible 2.1. Mind Maps:
A Tool to Determine Prior Knowledge

Mind Maps are often used to help students understand details. The following are some general guidelines for using Mind Maps:

1. The center circle represents the topic or the main idea.

2. The outer circles represent different attributes related to the topic or main idea.

3. Write each attribute in a different color.

4. Each attribute should have words and a visual (symbol or picture) to describe it. Using symbols and different colors helps the brain to store the information in a way that makes it easier to retrieve. Remember, the semantic memory system is not very reliable unless the information has a connector.

5. The descriptive attributes may require further clarification. If necessary, use arrows to connect more circles and show a relationship.

Sample Mind Map

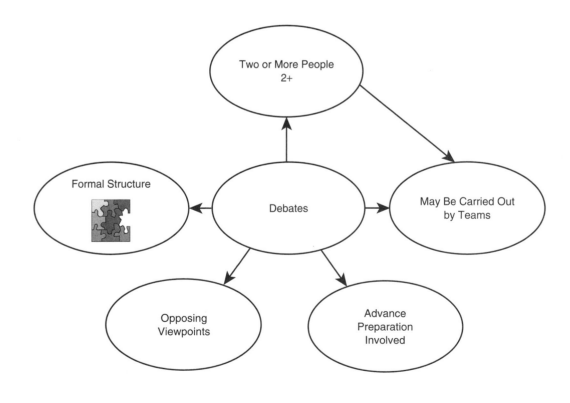

Reproducible 2.2. Similarities/Differences Organizer: A Tool for Understanding the Topics of the Learning

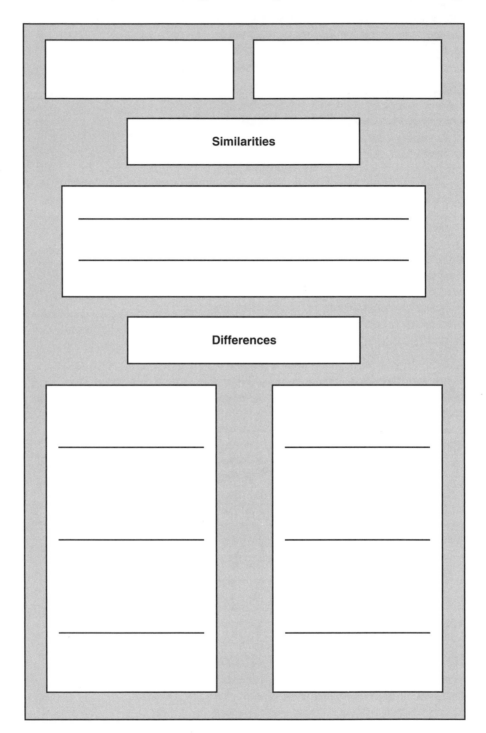

Reproducible 2.3. Four Corners Information Chart: A Tool for Dividing the Responsibility for the Learning

Directions: Fill out the Four Corners Information Chart based on your assigned chapter. Be prepared to share this information with the entire group.

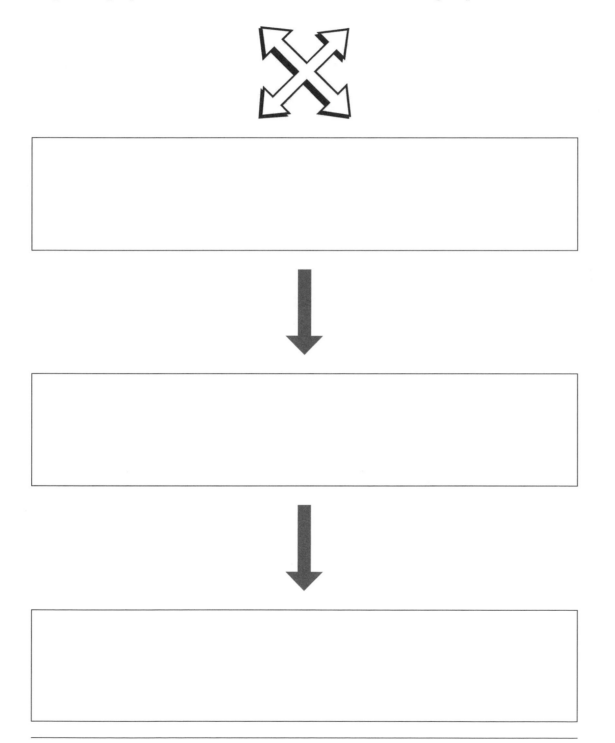

Reproducible 2.4. Student Motivation Survey: A Tool to Help Educators Determine Their Level of Understanding

Directions: For each topic, place an X in the Knowledge column that demonstrates your level of understanding. Next, rate your Confidence Level regarding each statement.

Importance of Student Motivation	*Knowledge*	
A. I understand the importance of student motivation to the learning process.	Yes	No

How confident are you? **Rate your level of confidence.**	**Rating Scale** (Place a check mark in the appropriate column) Not Confident Very Confident			
	1	**2**	**3**	**4**
1. I understand intrinsic motivation and its relationship to the learning process.				
2. I understand extrinsic motivation and its relationship to the learning process.				
3. I understand rewards and their relationship to the learning process.				
4. I understand celebrations and their relationship to the learning process.				
5. I understand the importance of the self-system and its relationship to student motivation.				
6. I understand the importance of the metacognitive system and its relationship to student motivation.				
7. I understand the importance of the cognitive system and its relationship to student motivation.				

The Brain and Student Motivation	*Knowledge*	
B. I understand the functioning of the brain and how it relates to student motivation.	Yes	No

How confident are you? **Rate your level of confidence.**	**Rating Scale** **(Place a check mark in** **the appropriate column)** Not Confident Very Confident			
	1	**2**	**3**	**4**
8. I understand the connection of emotion to student motivation.				
9. I understand how important locus of control is to student motivation.				
10. I understand how important relationships are to student motivation.				
11. I understand how threat can be detrimental to the learning process.				
12. I understand the components of climate and how they affect student motivation.				
13. I understand how to activate the metacognitive system to motivate students.				
14. I understand off-task behavior and how to redirect it.				

(Continued)

(Continued)

The Teacher and Student Motivation		Knowledge	
C. I understand the role of the teacher in student motivation.		Yes	No

How confident are you? Rate your level of confidence.	Rating Scale (Place a check mark in the appropriate column)			
	Not Confident			**Very Confident**
	1	**2**	**3**	**4**
15. I implement strategies that build relationships between the teacher and the students.				
16. I implement strategies that build relationships among students.				
17. I take steps to create a positive climate in the classroom.				
18. I implement strategies to access the self-system of the brain.				
19. I implement strategies to access the cognitive system of the brain.				
20. I implement strategies to access the metacognitive system of the brain.				

Reproducible 2.5. Model for Changing Demotivation to Motivation: A Tool for Putting the Learning Into Practice

Directions: For each statement, write what you will do in your classroom to help motivate learners.

I. Attitudes and Perceptions About the Learning

Category	What Will You Do?
Ensure students feel accepted by the teacher and by peers in the room	
Ensure students perceive the classroom as comfortable and orderly	
Ensure students experience the learning through the senses	
Ensure students are a part of the learning process	
Ensure that my grading procedures are fair and consistent	

II. The Self-System

Category	What Will You Do?
Routines for beginning class	
Importance of the task	
Efficacy	
Positive emotion	

III. The Metacognitive System

Category	What Will You Do?
Goal specification	
Process specification	
Process monitoring	
Deposition monitoring	

(Continued)

(Continued)

IV. Changing Temporary Learning States

Learning-State Problem	What Will You Do?
The activity	
The environment	
Mode of presentation	
People	
Tone	

V. Working With Diverse Learners

Diverse Learners	What Will You Do?
Inner-city learners	
Students from generational poverty	
English language learners	

SOURCE: Reprinted from *What Every Teacher Should Know About Student Motivation* by Donna Walker Tileston, Thousand Oaks, CA: Corwin Press, 2004. www.corwinpress.com

Reproducible 2.6. Three W's Chart:
Reflecting on the Learning

Directions: Answer each question regarding what you learned during this session.

```
What?




```

```
So What?




```

```
Now What?




```

Training Session 3

What Every Teacher Should Know About Learning, Memory, and the Brain

Learning is not a process left just to the brain; it involves the whole being. *What Every Teacher Should Know About Learning, Memory, and the Brain* examines how learning occurs and the implications for helping all students be successful. The book discusses factors that identify being smart and the factors that label students as "slow learners" or "overachievers." The book also examines the factors that help students take in information at a more efficient rate and the factors that help students retrieve information from long-term memory. Furthermore, the reader explores the tactics that help students learn and remember declarative knowledge and examines the importance of procedural tools. Finally, the book presents practical applications that help the reader make connections between the information on how learning occurs and ways to prepare and teach students effectively.

MATERIALS

You will need the following materials for this session:

A copy of *What Every Teacher Should Know About Learning, Memory, and the Brain* for each participant

Handouts for each participant

Transparencies of all reproducibles and an overhead projector (or other form of digital presentation)

Pens, pencils, markers, and highlighters

Chart paper

Tape, staples, pushpins, clips, or easels to display chart paper

Notepads or reusable notepaper

A CD player and music (recommended)

LEARNING OBJECTIVES

Declarative Objectives

Participants will know the following:

- How research about learning, memory, and the brain will help teachers make informed decisions about how to teach students
- The terminology related to learning, memory, and the brain
- How the brain processes and acquires information
- How meaning is constructed in the brain
- The long-term memory pathways of the semantic memory system, the episodic memory system, and the procedural memory system
- How to write declarative and procedural objectives
- How to help students construct meaning, organize information, store information, construct models, and internalize information

Procedural Objectives

Participants will be able to do the following:

- Create a Circle of Memory that details their knowledge of learning, memory, and the brain
- Define the terminology related to learning, memory, and the brain
- Assess their knowledge about learning, memory, and the brain
- Design a sign that promotes the acquisition and processing of information
- Relate to others how the brain acquires and processes information
- Construct a television commercial that defends the importance of the semantic memory system, the episodic memory system, the procedural memory system, and the construction of meaning in the brain
- Write declarative and procedural objectives
- Design a lesson that helps students construct meaning, organize information, store information, construct models, and internalize information

Suggested Activities and Time Frame

Estimated Time: 6 hours

Estimated Time on Task	Objectives	Activities
20 minutes	Declarative Objective— Participants willknow • How research about learning, memory, and the brain will help teachers make informed decisions about how to teach students.	**Activity 1: Preparing for the Learning** Invite the participants to form cooperative learning groups. Refer to Reproducible 0.1. Tell the participants that they will engage in a brainstorming activity to access prior knowledge. Share the rules of brainstorming on Reproducible 0.2. Display and model how to complete the Circle of Memory (Reproducible 3.1).
	Procedural Objective— Participants will be able to • Create a Circle of Memory that details their knowledge of learning, memory, and the brain	Give each group a sheet of chart paper. Ask the recorders to recreate the Circle of Memory on the chart paper. Instruct the groups to brainstorm everything they already know about learning, memory, and the brain. Tell the recorders to record the information in the smaller circles on the Circle of Memory. Tell them to add as many circles as necessary. Allow a few minutes for discussion, and then invite the reporters to post the charts and share their results with the large group. Introduce the topic of the workshop—*What Every Teacher Should Know About Learning, Memory, and the Brain.* Share the declarative and procedural objectives for the training. Refer the participants to the book *What Every Teacher Should Know About Learning, Memory, and the Brain.* Tell them that the activities in this workshop are designed to engage the participants in meaningful dialogue concerning learning, memory, and the brain.
45 minutes	Declarative Objective— Participants will know • The terminology related to learning, memory, and the brain.	**Activity 2: Examining the Vocabulary** Review and post the objectives for the activity. Remind the participants of the roles and guidelines for cooperative learning groups (see Reproducible 0.1).

(Continued)

(Continued)

Estimated Time on Task	Objectives	Activities
	Procedural Objective—Participants will be able to • Define the terminology related to learning, memory, and the brain.	Refer participants to the Vocabulary List for Assessment in *What Every Teacher Should Know About Learning, Memory, and the Brain* (p. xii). Instruct participants to provide a definition for each vocabulary word based on what they already know. Have them write their definitions in the column "Your Definition." Divide the vocabulary words equally among the groups. Ask the groups to discuss their assigned words, check the Vocabulary Summary, and review the text of the book to refine their definitions. Have them write the new definitions in the column "Your Revised Definition." Invite the reporters to share their revised definitions with the large group.
15 minutes	Procedural Objective—Participants will be able to • Assess their knowledge about learning, memory, and the brain.	**Pre-Test** Review and post the objective for the activity. Inform the group that it is important to assess the knowledge they bring to the workshop. At the conclusion of the workshop, they will be able to measure their learning and progress. Refer participants to the Vocabulary Pre-Test section of the book *What Every Teacher Should Know About Learning, Memory, and the Brain* (beginning on p. xiii). Have participants complete the test, and then direct them to the Post-Test Answer Key in the book *What Every Teacher Should Know About Learning, Memory, and the Brain* (p. 80). Ask participants to grade their tests and record the number of correct answers for future reference.
30–45 minutes	Declarative Objective—Participants will know • How the brain acquires and processes information.	**Activity 3: Making Use of the Information From the Book** *Part I—Acquiring and Processing Information* Review and post the objectives for the activity.

Estimated Time on Task	Objectives	Activities
	Procedural Objectives—Participants will be able to: • Design a sign that promotes acquiring and processing information. • Relate how the brain acquires and processes information to others.	Remind participants what they read about in Chapters 1 and 2 of *What Every Teacher Should Know About Learning, Memory, and the Brain.* Ask participants to form their cooperative learning groups. Briefly explain the importance of the brain in the learning process. Tell participants they are to create a sign that promotes the acquisition and processing of information in the brain. The sign will be directed at community members. Ask the materials keepers to retrieve colored markers and chart paper. Then, prompt the groups to design and create a sign to be placed in the community that promotes the acquisition and processing of information. When groups have completed their signs, instruct the reporters to post them around the room. Direct the participants to walk around the room to examine the signs. (You may want to play some music while people move around the room.) Allow several minutes for people to look, and then assemble the large group back together. Hold a brief discussion about any new insights.
30–45 minutes	Declarative Objectives—Participants will know • How meaning is constructed in the brain. • The long-term memory pathways of the semantic memory system, the episodic memory system, and the procedural memory system.	**Activity 3: Making Use of the Information From the Book** *Part II—Memory* Review and post the objectives for the activity. Remind the participants of the roles and guidelines for cooperative learning groups (see Reproducible 0.1). Divide the participants into four groups. If four groups are not possible, select the most appropriate topics from those described below.
	Procedural Objectives—Participants will be able to: • Construct a television	Ask participants to refer to Chapters 3 and 4 of the book *What Every Teacher Should Know About Learning, Memory, and the Brain.* Assign one of the following topics to each group: The Semantic Memory System, The Episodic

(Continued)

Estimated Time on Task	Objectives	Activities
	commercial that defends the importance of the semantic memory system, the episodic memory system, the procedural memory system, and the construction of meaning in the brain.	Memory System, The Procedural Memory System, and Constructing Meaning. Direct each group to create a 30-second television commercial that defends the importance of their topic to learning and the brain. Once each group has created and rehearsed its commercial, invite the groups to present their commercials. You can even videotape the presentations and play them at another session.
35 minutes	Procedural Objective—Participants will be able to • Assess their knowledge about learning, memory, and the brain.	**Activity 4: Knowledge and Confidence** Review and post the objective for the activity. Tell the participants that they have reviewed the vocabulary, read the book, and actively discussed the topics of learning, memory, and the brain. Ask them to assess their knowledge and confidence in applying the information they have learned. Make a copy of Reproducible 3.2, the Learning, Memory, and the Brain Survey, for each participant. Have them complete the survey individually. Then, in their learning groups, encourage participants to discuss the results and create a chart of new knowledge and insights. Invite the reporters to share the lists with the large group.
20 minutes	Declarative Objectives—Participants will know • How to write declarative and procedural objectives. • How to help students construct meaning, organize information, store information, construct models, and internalize information.	**Activity 5: Practical Application in the Classroom** Review and post the objectives for the activity. Inform participants that they will be planning a lesson for their classes. Urge the participants to refer to Chapters 5 and 6 of the book *What Every Teacher Should Know About Learning, Memory, and the Brain.* If necessary, host a brief discussion to review key learning points and vocabulary from the book. Then, display and model how to complete The Lesson-Planning Outline found

Estimated Time on Task	Objectives	Activities
	Procedural Objectives— Participants will be able to • Write declarative and procedural objectives. • Design a lesson that helps students construct meaning, organize information, store information, construct models, and internalize information.	on Reproducible 3.3. Direct participants to complete their own outlines for a lesson plan they will use in their classrooms. Provide guidance and answer questions as necessary. Note: If the workshop is being conducted in multiple sessions, you can dismiss participants to create their lesson-plan outlines. Announce a date and time for the next session, at which members will share their lesson plans. If the workshop is conducted in a one- or two-day session, have participants complete imaginary lesson-plan outlines during the session and share their ideas within their groups.
45 minutes	Procedural Objective— Participants will be able to • Assess their knowledge about learning, memory, and the brain.	**Activity 6: Self-Evaluation** Review and post the objective for the activity. Direct participants to share their lesson-plan outlines (from Activity 5) within their learning groups. Prompt participants to complete the Vocabulary Post-Test beginning on page 75 in the book *What Every Teacher Should Know About Learning, Memory, and the Brain*. Have participants grade their Post-Tests and record the number of correct responses. Then, ask them to compare the results to the Pre-Test.
45 minutes	Procedural Objective— Participants will be able to • Assess their knowledge about learning, memory, and the brain.	**Activity 7: Reflection** Review and post the objective for the activity. Review the Three W's Chart (Reproducible 3.4) with participants. Ask them to complete the Three W's Chart on their own, and then discuss individual responses within their cooperative groups. Ask the reporters to share any new insights with the large group. If appropriate, have the participants complete the Facilitator Evaluation Survey (Reproducible 0.3) for the training.

Reproducible 3.1. Circle of Memory:
A Brainstorming Activity to Determine Prior Learning

Directions: Brainstorm everything you know about learning, memory, and the brain. Write words or phrases in the circles. Add circles as necessary.

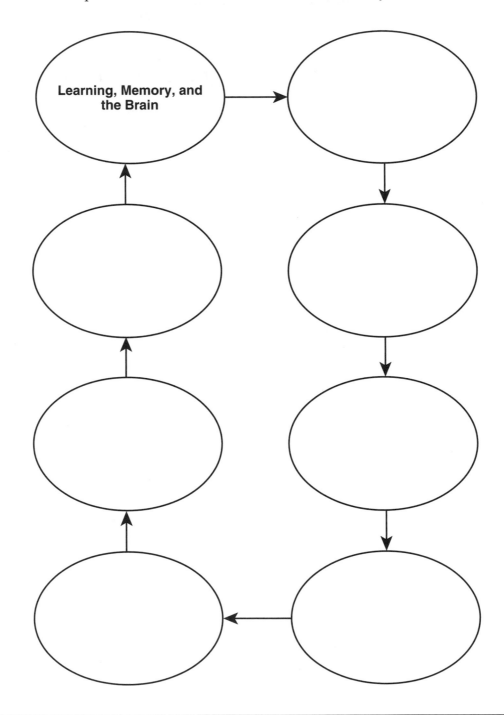

___

Reproducible 3.2. Learning, Memory, and the Brain Survey: A Tool to Help Educators Determine Their Level of Understanding

Directions: For each topic, place an X in the Knowledge column that demonstrates your level of understanding. Next, rate your Confidence Level regarding each statement.

Acquiring and Processing Information	*Knowledge*	
A. I understand how the brain acquires and processes information.	Yes	No

How confident are you? Rate your level of confidence.	Rating Scale (Place a check mark in the appropriate column) Not Confident Very Confident			
	1	**2**	**3**	**4**
1. I understand the importance of the self-system to the learning process.				
2. I understand the importance of the metacognitive system to the learning process.				
3. I understand the importance of the cognitive system to the learning process.				
4. I understand how differing learning modalities are important to processing information.				
5. I am familiar with the perceptual register or reticular activation system (RAS) and how it helps the brain deal with incoming data.				
6. I understand rote and elaborative rehearsal and use both appropriately.				
7. I understand the information processing functions of the brain.				

(Continued)

(Continued)

Memory		*Knowledge*	
B. I understand the memory systems of the brain.		Yes	No
How confident are you? **Rate your level of confidence.**	**Rating Scale** **(Place a check mark in the appropriate column)** Not Confident Very Confident		
	1	2	3	4
8. I understand the semantic memory system.				
9. I understand how to increase the ability of the semantic memory system to hold information.				
10. I understand how to help students retrieve information from the semantic memory system.				
11. I understand the episodic memory system.				
12. I understand how to help students activate the episodic memory system.				
13. I understand the procedural memory system.				
14. I understand how to help students activate the procedural memory system.				

Declarative and Procedural		Knowledge	
C. I understand the importance of declarative and procedural knowledge.		Yes	No

How confident are you? Rate your level of confidence.	Rating Scale (Place a check mark in the appropriate column)			
	Not Confident			Very Confident
	1	2	3	4
15. I can write appropriate declarative objectives for my students.				
16. I can write appropriate procedural objectives for my students.				
17. I implement strategies that help my students construct meaning from the learning.				
18. I implement strategies that help students make connections with declarative information.				
19. I implement strategies that help students construct mental models, shape information, and make learned skills automatic.				
20. I understand how to implement strategies that have the strongest probability of helping at-risk learners utilize long-term memory pathways.				

Reproducible 3.3. The Lesson-Planning Outline: A Tool to Help Teachers Plan Brain Compatible Lessons

Directions: Choose a lesson that you will soon teach in your classroom. For that lesson, answer the following questions using what you learned from the book *What Every Teacher Should Know About Learning, Memory, and the Brain.*

Step 1

List the state learning objective (or standard) for the lesson.

_____

_____

_____

_____

Step 2

List the declarative and procedural objective(s) for the lesson (what students will know and be able to do).

Declarative:

_____

_____

_____

_____

Procedural:

_____

_____

_____

_____

Step 3

How will I help students construct meaning?

_____

_____

_____

_____

Step 4

How will I help students organize the information?

_____

_____

_____

_____

Step 5

How will I help students store the information?

_____

_____

_____

_____

Step 6

How will I help students construct models?

_____

_____

_____

_____

(Continued)

(Continued)

Step 7

How will I help students internalize information?

_____

_____

_____

_____

Reproducible 3.4. Three W's Chart: Reflecting on the Learning

Directions: Answer each question regarding what you learned during this session.

```
What?




```

```
So What?




```

```
Now What?




```

Training Session 4

What Every Teacher Should Know About Instructional Planning

Wiggins and McTighe (1998) identify a three-step process in planning for instruction. Three important questions are explored in *What Every Teacher Should Know About Instructional Planning* to help teachers through the process: (a) What do we want students to know and be able to do as a result of the learning? (b) How will we know that our students are learning and that they can perform tasks as a result of the learning? and (c) Which instructional practices will assure us that students learn and that they can use the information provided?

MATERIALS

You will need the following materials for this session:

A copy of *What Every Teacher Should Know About Instructional Planning* for each participant

Handouts for each participant

Transparencies of all reproducibles and an overhead projector (or other form of digital presentation)

Pens, pencils, markers, and highlighters

Chart paper

Tape, staples, pushpins, clips, or easels to display chart paper

Notepads or reusable notepaper

A CD player and music (recommended)

A copy of the state academic standards

LEARNING OBJECTIVES

Declarative Objectives

Participants will know the following:

- The terminology related to instructional planning
- The principles of planning
- The components of state standards
- The appropriate use of declarative objectives
- The appropriate use of procedural objectives
- Activities related to evidencing learning
- Activities related to planning meaningful learning experiences
- The steps in the planning process

Procedural Objectives

Participants will be able to do the following:

- Define the terminology related to instructional planning
- Identify the principles of planning
- Describe the use of standards as a guide
- List the key components of declarative objectives
- List the key components of procedural objectives
- Create a Learning Log related to planning and evidencing meaningful learning experiences
- Assess their knowledge about the instructional planning within the school
- Plan a lesson utilizing the steps for planning a lesson
- Assess their knowledge of instructional planning

Suggested Activities and Time Frame

Estimated Time: 6 hours

Estimated Time on Task	Objectives	Activities
45 minutes	Declarative Objective—Participants will know • Vocabulary related to instructional planning.	**Activity 1: Preparing for the Learning** Invite the participants to form cooperative learning groups. Refer to Reproducible 0.1. Display and model how to complete the What Do I Know? chart (Reproducible 4.1). Show participants how to identify what they already know about the topics and give a brief description of what they know. Give participants a copy of the handout and ask them to complete it individually. Later, have them discuss it with the group. Tell the participants that at the end of the workshop they will revisit the chart to assess their new level of knowledge. Remind participants to keep it for future use. Introduce the topic of the workshop—*What Every Teacher Should Know About Instructional Planning.* Share the declarative and procedural objectives for the training. Refer the participants to the book *What Every Teacher Should Know About Instructional Planning.* Tell them that the activities in this workshop are designed to engage the participants in meaningful dialogue concerning instructional planning.
45 minutes	Declarative Objective—Participants will know • The terminology related to instructional planning. Procedural Objective—Participants will be able to • Define the terminology related to instructional planning.	**Activity 2: Examining the Vocabulary** Review and post the objectives for the activity. Remind the participants of the roles and guidelines for cooperative learning groups (Reproducible 0.1). Refer participants to the Vocabulary List for Assessment in *What Every Teacher Should Know About Instructional Planning* (pp. xiii–xiv). Instruct participants to provide a definition for each vocabulary word based on what they already know. Have them write their definitions in the column "Your Definition."

(Continued)

(Continued)

Estimated Time on Task	Objectives	Activities
		Divide the vocabulary words equally among the groups. Ask the groups to discuss their assigned words, check the Vocabulary Summary, and review the text of the book to refine their definitions. Have them write the new definitions in the column "Your Revised Definition."
		Invite the reporters to share their revised definitions with the large group.
15 minutes	Procedural Objective— Participants will be able to • Assess their knowledge about instructional planning.	**Pre-Test** Review and post the objective for the activity. Inform the group that it is important to assess the knowledge they bring to the workshop. At the conclusion of the workshop, they will be able to measure their learning and progress. Refer participants to the Vocabulary Pre-Test section of the book *What Every Teacher Should Know About Instructional Planning* (beginning on p. xv). Have participants complete the test, and then direct them to the Post-Test Answer Key in the book *What Every Teacher Should Know About Instructional Planning* (p. 99). Ask participants to grade their tests and record the number of correct answers for future reference.
30–45 minutes	Declarative Objectives— Participants will know • The principles of planning. • The components of state standards. • The appropriate use of declarative objectives. • The appropriate use of procedural objectives.	**Activity 3: Making Use of the Information From the Book** *Part I—Understanding What Students Need to Know and Be Able to Do* Review and post the objectives for the activity. Refer participants to Chapters 1–4 of *What Every Teacher Should Know About Instructional Planning*. Note: Participants will not form their usual cooperative groups. Have all participants form a large circle around the room. Ask them to

Estimated Time on Task	Objectives	Activities
	Procedural Objectives— Participants will be able to • Identify the principles of planning. • Describe the use of standards as a guide. • List the key components of declarative objectives. • List the key components of procedural objectives.	number off from 1 to 4, so that you have four groups with approximately the same number of people. Direct all the 1s to one corner of the room, the 2s to another corner of the room, and so on. The four groups should be in opposing corners of the room.
		Tell each group what their topic will be: *Group 1:* Chapter 1 *Group 2:* Chapter 2 *Group 3:* Chapter 3 *Group 4:* Chapter 4
		Within their groups, prompt participants to review their assigned chapter of the book *What Every Teacher Should Know About Instructional Planning* and discuss what they have learned. Make a copy of the Four Corners Information Chart (Reproducible 4.2) for each group. Instruct someone to recreate the chart onto chart paper. After the groups hold their discussions, tell the recorder to write down the three key learning points and the significant implications in the appropriate places on the chart. Finally, have the groups post their charts on a wall in their respective corners.
		Show participants how to move, as a group, to each corner of the room. (You may want to play music while people are moving about the room.) At each corner, encourage participants to reflect on the key points and significant implications from the other chapters.
		When everyone has had a chance to review all four corners, host a large group discussion to debrief the results.
30–45 minutes	Declarative Objectives— Participants will know • Activities related to evidencing learning. • Activities related to planning meaningful learning experiences.	**Activity 3: Making Use of the Information From the Book** *Part II—Planning and Gathering Evidence of Meaningful Learning* Review and post the objectives for the activity. Remind the participants of the roles and guidelines for cooperative learning groups (Reproducible 0.1).

(Continued)

(Continued)

Estimated Time on Task	Objectives	Activities
	Procedural Objective—Participants will be able to • Create a Learning Log related to planning and evidencing meaningful learning experiences.	Give each participant a copy of the Learning Log (Reproducible 4.3). Display and model how to complete the Learning Log. Refer the participants to Chapters 5 and 6 of the book *What Every Teacher Should Know About Instructional Planning*. Instruct the participants to choose one of those chapters to study. Prompt participants to quote important phrases or passages from the chapter on the left side of the Learning Log. On the right side of the Learning Log, have them write down their thoughts about each quote. Allow several minutes for individuals to work, and then invite the participants to join their learning groups. Encourage the groups to share their work and discuss the key learning points from the chapters. Finally, invite the reporters to reveal the highlights of the discussion with the large group.
35 minutes	Procedural Objective—Participants will be able to • Assess their knowledge about the instructional planning within the school.	**Activity 4: Knowledge and Confidence** Review and post the objective for the activity. Tell the participants that they have reviewed the vocabulary, read the book, and actively discussed the topic of instructional planning. Ask them to assess their knowledge and confidence in applying the information they have learned. Make a copy of the Instructional Planning Survey (Reproducible 4.4) for each participant. Have them complete the survey individually. Then, in their learning groups, encourage participants to discuss the results and create a chart of new knowledge and insights. Invite the reporters to share the lists with the large group.
20 minutes	Declarative Objective—Participants will know • The steps in the planning process.	**Activity 5: Practical Application in the Classroom** Review and post the objectives for the activity.

Estimated Time on Task	Objectives	Activities
	Procedural Objective— Participants will be able to • Plan a lesson utilizing the steps for planning a lesson.	Note: Inform the participants prior to the session that they will need to bring a copy of the state standards and any other necessary resources to plan a lesson for their classrooms. Ask participants to review Chapter 8 of the book *What Every Teacher Should Know About Instructional Planning.* Make a copy of the Lesson Plan Template (Reproducible 4.5) for each participant. Have each teacher plan a lesson utilizing the steps outlined in Chapter 8 and given on the handout. Note: If the workshop is being conducted in multiple sessions, you can ask the participants to complete the lesson plan at their discretion. Encourage participants to record their reactions to the process in a professional journal. During subsequent sessions, invite participants to share their lesson plans and request more guidance, if necessary. If the workshop is conducted in a one- or two-day session, have participants complete a shortened version of the plan during the session and share their ideas within their groups.
45 minutes	Procedural Objective— Participants will • Assess their knowledge of instructional planning.	**Activity 6: Self-Evaluation** Review and post the objective for the activity. Direct participants to share their lesson plans (from Activity 5) within their learning groups. Prompt participants to complete the Vocabulary Post-Test beginning on page 95 in the book *What Every Teacher Should Know About Instructional Planning.* Have participants grade their Post-Tests and record the number of correct responses. Then, ask them to compare the results to the Pre-Test.
45 minutes	Procedural Objective— Participants will be able to • Assess their knowledge of instructional planning.	**Activity 7: Reflection** Review and post the objective for the activity. Remind the participants about the activity they completed at the beginning of this session. Ask them to retrieve the What Do I Know? handout (Reproducible 4.1). Have

(Continued)

(Continued)

Estimated Time on Task	Objectives	Activities
		them review their responses from the beginning of the workshop and make any changes that incorporate their new knowledge.
		Give each group a sheet of chart paper. Prompt the participants to discuss what they have learned within their groups. Encourage the recorders to compile lists of new insights and write them on the chart paper. Invite the reporters to share the lists with the large group.
		If appropriate, have the participants complete the Facilitator Evaluation Survey (Reproducible 0.3) for the training.

Reproducible 4.1. What Do I Know?: A Tool for Determining Prior Knowledge

Directions: At the beginning of the session, mark an X in the column that best describes your current level of knowledge. Then, write a brief description of what you know about the topic.

At the end of the session, review your responses. Compare what you knew at the beginning to what you now know. Make any adjustments on the chart to incorporate your new knowledge.

Word	Know It Well	Have Heard It/Seen It	Don't Know It
Declarative Objectives			
Procedural Objectives			
Mental Models			
Shaping Information			
Automaticity			
Storing Information			
Benchmarks			

Reproducible 4.2. Four Corners Information Chart: A Tool for Synthesizing and Debriefing Information

Directions: Fill out the Four Corners Information Chart based on your assigned chapter. Be prepared to share this information with the entire group.

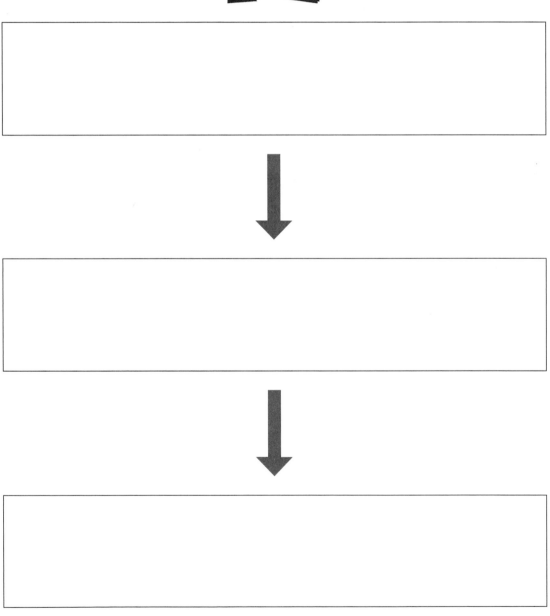

Reproducible 4.3. Learning Log:
A Tool for Reflecting on the Learning

Directions: On the left side of the log, write important phrases or passages from the chapters assigned. On the right side of the page, write your thoughts on each passage.

Passages	My Thoughts

Reproducible 4.4. Instructional Planning Survey: A Tool to Help Educators Determine Their Level of Understanding

Directions: For each topic, place an X in the Knowledge column that demonstrates your level of understanding. Next, rate your Confidence Level regarding each statement.

Principles of Planning	*Knowledge*	
A. I understand the basic principles of instructional planning.	Yes	No

How confident are you? Rate your level of confidence.	**Rating Scale (Place a check mark in the appropriate column)**			
	Not Confident			**Very Confident**
	1	**2**	**3**	**4**
1. I understand how planning relates to learning experiences.				
2. I understand the sequential steps in the process of planning for instruction.				
3. I have examined my state standards for instruction.				
4. I understand how to analyze and use my state standards for instruction.				
5. I know how to construct declarative objectives.				
6. I know how to construct procedural objectives.				
7. I can devise activities to help students organize declarative knowledge.				
8. I can devise activities to help students store declarative knowledge.				
9. I understand the three parallel steps of procedural knowledge.				
10. I can construct activities to assist my students in utilizing procedural knowledge.				

Planning and Evidencing Meaningful Learning		Knowledge	
B. I understand how to plan and assess learning.		Yes	No
How confident are you? **Rate your level of confidence.**	**Rating Scale** (Place a check mark in the appropriate column) Not Confident Very Confident		
	1	2	3	4

How confident are you? Rate your level of confidence.	1	2	3	4
11. I design activities that tell students what I expect and how I will grade their work.				
12. I devise activities that demonstrate students have met learning standards.				
13. I understand how to create performance tasks that provide evidence of learning.				
14. I understand how to create rubrics to assess the level of student learning.				
15. I design activities aligned to state learning standards.				
16. I design activities that link old and new knowledge.				
17. I construct activities to assist students in organizing information.				
18. I construct activities to assist students in storing information.				
19. I design activities to help students shape and internalize procedural knowledge.				

(Continued)

(Continued)

Planning Into Action	Knowledge	
C. I know and can use the key steps in the process of planning for instruction.	Yes	No

How confident are you? Rate your level of confidence.	Rating Scale (Place a check mark in the appropriate column)			
	Not Confident			Very Confident
	1	2	3	4
20. I can describe the steps involved in planning for instruction.				
21. I understand how to analyze state learning standards and decide what to teach using the standards provided.				
22. I understand how to analyze state standards to assist me in writing declarative objectives.				
23. I understand how to analyze state standards to assist me in writing procedural objectives.				
24. I know how to use declarative and procedural objectives as a guide for developing assessments.				

Reproducible 4.5. Lesson Plan Template

Directions: Review Chapter 8 in the book *What Every Teacher Should Know About Instructional Planning*. Plan a lesson following the steps below.

Steps 1 and 2

List the state standard and any benchmarks for your lesson.

Step 3

List the key concept(s), facts, and so forth for what you are going to be teaching.

Step 4

Write your Declarative Objectives for this lesson.

(Continued)

(Continued)

Step 5

Write your Procedural Objectives for this lesson.

```



```

Step 6

List how you will assess student learning (e.g., by using a rubric).

```



```

Steps 7 and 8

Describe how you will inform parents and students of the learning objectives.

```



```

Step 9

Describe how you will lead students in writing personal learning goals.

```



```

Step 10

Write the lesson by following the questions below.

- How will students construct declarative information?

- How will students organize declarative information?

- How will students store declarative information?

- How will students construct models for the procedural information?

- How will students use shaping for procedural information?

- How will students internalize procedural information?

Step 11

List the materials you will need for this lesson.

Step 12

Describe how you will evaluate student learning.

Training Session 5

What Every Teacher Should Know About Effective Teaching Strategies

M uch is said about the alignment of curriculum to assessment, but little is written about the alignment of instructional strategies to curriculum and assessment. Once we know the standards, the benchmarks for our subject or grade level, and our own objectives, how do we decide which instructional tools will make the most difference in student learning? Now we have research that allows us to make better decisions about the "how" of teaching. *What Every Teacher Should Know About Effective Teaching Strategies* describes the learning process and research concerning instructional tools. In it, lesson planning is analyzed and graphic organizers and verbal tools are explained.

MATERIALS

You will need the following materials for this session:

A copy of *What Every Teacher Should Know About Effective Teaching Strategies* for each participant

Handouts for each participant

Transparencies of all reproducibles and an overhead projector (or other form of digital presentation)

Pens, pencils, markers, and highlighters

Chart paper

Tape, staples, pushpins, clips, or easels to display chart paper

Notepads or reusable notepaper

Index cards

A CD player and music (recommended)

A copy of the state academic standards

LEARNING OBJECTIVES

Declarative Objectives

Participants will know the following:

- What teaching strategies are currently used in the classroom
- The terminology related to effective teaching strategies
- The key learning points found in Chapters 1–4 of *What Every Teacher Should Know About Effective Teaching Strategies*
- The name, purpose, and classroom application of the list of organizers and verbal tools
- The relationship among state standards, declarative objectives, and procedural objectives
- How to utilize a variety of graphic organizers and verbal tools in the classroom

Procedural Objectives

Participants will be able to do the following:

- Create a list of teaching strategies used in the classroom
- Define the terminology related to effective teaching strategies
- Assess their knowledge about effective teaching strategies
- Complete a Chapter Debriefing Chart on the key learning points found in each section of Chapters 1–4 of *What Every Teacher Should Know About Effective Teaching Strategies*
- List key learning points found in Chapters 1–4 of *What Every Teacher Should Know About Effective Teaching Strategies*
- Report key learning points found in Chapters 1–4 of *What Every Teacher Should Know About Effective Teaching Strategies*
- Describe the purpose and classroom application of each organizer or verbal tool that was assigned
- List state, declarative, and procedural objectives
- Design and use a graphic organizer or verbal tool in a lesson
- Explain the use of a graphic organizer or verbal tool

Suggested Activities and Time Frame

Estimated Time: 6 hours

Estimated Time on Task	Objectives	Activities
20 minutes	Declarative Objective—Participants will know • What teaching strategies are currently used in the classroom. Procedural Objective—Participants will be able to • Create a list of teaching strategies used in the classroom.	**Activity 1: Preparing for the Learning** Invite the participants to form cooperative learning groups. Refer to Reproducible 0.1. Tell the participants that they will engage in a brainstorming activity to access prior knowledge. Share the rules of brainstorming on Reproducible 0.2. Display and model how to complete the Light Bulb activity using Reproducible 5.1. Give each participant a copy of the Light Bulb handout. Tell them to brainstorm all the teaching strategies they currently use in the classroom. Then, ask them to give reasons why these strategies have been successful. Allow several minutes for the participants to brainstorm. Then, ask them to share within their learning groups. Prompt the groups to select three strategies from the discussion that they feel are most effective in promoting student learning. Encourage them to discuss why these strategies are effective. Invite the reporters to present the information to the large group. Introduce the topic of the workshop—*What Every Teacher Should Know About Effective Teaching Strategies.* Share the declarative and procedural objectives for the training. Refer the participants to the book *What Every Teacher Should Know About Effective Teaching Strategies.* Tell them that the activities in this workshop are designed to engage the participants in meaningful dialogue concerning effective teaching strategies.
45 minutes	Declarative Objective—Participants will know • The terminology related to effective teaching strategies.	**Activity 2: Examining the Vocabulary** Review and post the objectives for the activity. Remind the participants of the roles and guidelines for cooperative learning groups (see Reproducible 0.1).

(Continued)

(Continued)

Estimated Time on Task	Objectives	Activities
	Procedural Objective— Participants will be able to • Define the terminology related to effective teaching strategies.	Refer participants to the Vocabulary List for Assessment in *What Every Teacher Should Know About Effective Teaching Strategies* (p. xiii). Instruct participants to provide a definition for each vocabulary word based on what they already know. Have them write their definitions in the column "Your Definition." Divide the vocabulary words equally among the groups. Ask the groups to discuss their assigned words, check the Vocabulary Summary, and review the text of the book to refine their definitions. Have them write the new definitions in the column "Your Revised Definition." Invite the reporters to share their revised definitions with the large group.
15 minutes	Procedural Objective— Participants will be able to • Assess their knowledge about effective teaching strategies.	**Pre-Test** Review and post the objective for the activity. Inform the group that it is important to assess the knowledge they bring to the workshop. At the conclusion of the workshop, they will be able to measure their learning and progress. Refer participants to the Vocabulary Pre-Test section of the book *What Every Teacher Should Know About Effective Teaching Strategies* (beginning on p. xv). Have participants complete the test, and then direct them to the Post-Test Answer Key in the book *What Every Teacher Should Know About Effective Teaching Strategies* (p. 107). Ask participants to grade their tests and record the number of correct answers for future reference.
30–45 minutes	Declarative Objective— Participants will know • The key learning points found in Chapters 1–4 of *What Every Teacher Should Know About Effective Teaching Strategies*.	**Activity 3: Making Use of the Information From the Book** *Part I—Effective Teaching Strategies: Chapters 1–4* Review and post the objectives for the activity. Remind the participants of the roles and guidelines for cooperative learning groups (see Reproducible 0.1).

Estimated Time on Task	Objectives	Activities
	Procedural Objectives— Participants will be able to • Complete a Chapter Debriefing Chart on the key learning points found in each section of Chapters 1–4 of *What Every Teacher Should Know About Effective Teaching Strategies*. • List key learning points found in Chapters 1–4 of *What Every Teacher Should Know About Effective Teaching Strategies*. • Report key learning points found in Chapters 1–4 of *What Every Teacher Should Know About Effective Teaching Strategies*.	Refer the participants to Chapters 1–4 of the book *What Every Teacher Should Know About Effective Teaching Strategies*. Write the chapter numbers 1 through 4 on index cards. Shuffle the cards and give one card to the pilot of each group. Tell the pilots that they will lead their groups through reading that chapter. (If you do not have four cooperative groups, reassign some participants to create four groups.) Make a copy of Reproducible 5.2 for each participant. Tell the pilots to assign a section(s) of their chapter to group members. Then, have the group members read their assigned sections and complete the Chapter Debriefing Sheet (Reproducible 5.2). Prompt the recorders to summarize the important learning points on a sheet of chart paper. Finally, invite the reporters to present the summaries to the large group.
30–45 minutes	Declarative Objective— Participants will know • The name, purpose, and classroom application of the list of organizers and verbal tools. Procedural Objective— Participants will be able to • Describe the purpose and classroom application of each organizer or verbal tool that was assigned.	**Activity 3: Making Use of the Information From the Book** *Part II—Graphic Organizers and Verbal Tools* Review and post the objectives for the activity. Remind the participants of the roles and guidelines for cooperative learning groups (see Reproducible 0.1). Refer participants to Chapters 4 and 5 of the book *What Every Teacher Should Know About Effective Teaching Strategies*. Reproducibles 5.3 and 5.4 list 16 graphic organizers and verbal tools described in the book *What Every Teacher Should Know About Effective Teaching Strategies*. Divide the organizers and tools as evenly as possible among the groups.

(Continued)

(Continued)

Estimated Time on Task	Objectives	Activities
		Instruct the groups to explain the purpose and application for each of the organizers and verbal tools they have been given.
		When everyone is finished, ask the reporters to share the name, purpose, and classroom application for each organizer or tool the group was assigned. Prompt participants to complete the chart on the handout while they are listening.
35 minutes	Procedural Objective— Participants will be able to • Assess their knowledge about effective teaching strategies.	**Activity 4: Knowledge and Confidence** Review and post the objective for the activity. Tell the participants that they have reviewed the vocabulary, read the book, and actively discussed the topic of effective teaching strategies. Ask them to assess their knowledge and confidence in applying the information they have learned. Make a copy of the Effective Teaching Strategies Survey (Reproducible 5.5) for each participant. Have them complete the survey individually. Then, in their learning groups, encourage participants to discuss the results and create a chart of new knowledge and insights. Invite the reporters to share the lists with the large group.
20 minutes	Declarative Objectives— Participants will know • The relationship among state, declarative, and procedural objectives. • How to utilize a variety of graphic organizers and verbal tools in the classroom. Procedural Objectives— Participants will be able to • List state, declarative, and procedural objectives.	**Activity 5: Assignment for the Classroom** Review and post the objectives for the activity. Display and model how to complete the Tools for the Classroom form using Reproducible 5.6. Direct the participants to complete the Tools for the Classroom worksheet for an upcoming lesson. Note: If the workshop is being conducted in multiple sessions, you can ask the participants to complete the worksheet at their discretion. Encourage participants to record their progress with the lesson plan by keeping a journal, collecting evidence, or videotaping their classrooms. During subsequent sessions, invite participants to share their success and request more guidance. If the workshop is conducted in a one- or two-day session, have

Estimated Time on Task	Objectives	Activities
	• Design and use a graphic organizer or verbal tool in a lesson. • Explain the use of a graphic organizer or verbal tool.	participants complete the worksheet using a theoretical lesson and share their ideas within their groups. However, the worksheet should be completed by each participant individually.
45 minutes	Procedural Objective—Participants will be able to • Assess their knowledge about effective teaching strategies.	**Activity 6: Self-Evaluation** Review and post the objective for the activity. Direct participants to share their Tools for the Classroom worksheet (from Activity 5) within their learning groups. Prompt participants to complete the Vocabulary Post-Test beginning on page 103 in the book *What Every Teacher Should Know About Effective Teaching Strategies*. Have participants grade their Post-Tests and record the number of correct responses. Then, ask them to compare the results to the Pre-Test.
45 minutes	Procedural Objective—Participants will be able to • Assess their knowledge about effective teaching strategies.	**Activity 7: Reflection** Review and post the objective for the activity. Display and model how to complete the PMI (Positive-Minus-Interesting) Chart (Reproducible 5.7). Have each participant complete a PMI Chart individually. Then, instruct the groups to complete a group PMI Chart that contains a consensus of the most significant thoughts for each category. When the groups have completed their discussions, ask the reporters to share with the large group. If appropriate, have the participants complete the Facilitator Evaluation Survey (Reproducible 0.3) for the training.

Reproducible 5.1. Light Bulb: A Tool for Brainstorming

Directions: Describe several effective strategies you use in your classroom. Provide reasons why these strategies are successful.

Reproducible 5.2. Chapter Debriefing Sheet: A Tool for Summarizing Information

Chapter Number _____

Section Title _____

Key Learning Points:

-
-
-
-
-
-
-
-
-
-

Reproducible 5.3. Graphic Organizers—The Facts: A Procedural Tool to Facilitate Teaching Declarative Information

Directions: Explain the purpose and application for each item.

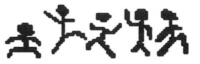

Name	Purpose	Classroom Application
KWLH		
Prediction Tree		
Flow Chart		
Before & After		
Branching Patterns		
Sequence/Interval Patterns		
Process/Cause Patterns		
Problem/Solution Patterns		
Generalization Patterns		
Compare/Contrast Patterns		

Reproducible 5.4. Verbal Tools—The Facts: A Tool to Facilitate Understanding of the Learning

Name	Purpose	Classroom Application
Brainstorming		
Socratic Questioning		
Quaker Dialogues		
PMI		
Three W's Chart		
Ticket Out the Door		

Reproducible 5.5. Effective Teaching Strategies Survey: A Tool to Help Educators Determine Their Level of Understanding

Directions: For each topic, place an X in the Knowledge column that demonstrates your level of understanding. Next, rate your Confidence Level regarding each statement.

Effective Teaching Strategies and the Brain	*Knowledge*	
A. I understand the connection between effective teaching strategies and the brain.	Yes	No

How confident are you? **Rate your level of confidence.**	**Rating Scale** (Place a check mark in the appropriate column) Not Confident Very Confident			
	1	2	3	4
1. I have a clear understanding of the self-system and its relationship to effective teaching strategies.				
2. I have a clear understanding of the metacognitive system and its relationship to effective teaching strategies.				
3. I have a clear understanding of the cognitive system and its relationship to effective teaching strategies.				
4. I understand the importance of rehearsal for storage and retrieval of information in the brain.				
5. I understand memory pathways and how to create effective teaching strategies that utilize these pathways.				

(Continued)

(Continued)

Effective Teaching Strategies and Planning		*Knowledge*	
B. I understand the connection between effective teaching strategies and planning.		Yes	No

How confident are you? **Rate your level of confidence.**	**Rating Scale** **(Place a check mark in** **the appropriate column)**			
	Not Confident			**Very Confident**
	1	**2**	**3**	**4**
6. I understand the importance of and how to create a positive classroom climate.				
7. I understand the differing structures that must be in place in order for students to be successful.				
8. I understand how to introduce a lesson or unit to students.				
9. I understand to hook my students into the learning.				
10. I understand how to make learning relevant.				
11. I understand how to write declarative and procedural objectives.				

Effective Teaching Strategies: Graphic Organizers/Verbal Tools	Knowledge	
C. I understand how to utilize graphic organizers and verbal tools in classroom instruction.	Yes	No

How confident are you? Rate your level of confidence.	Rating Scale (Place a check mark in the appropriate column)			
	Not Confident			Very Confident
	1	2	3	4
12. I use graphic organizers to access prior knowledge.				
13. I understand how to help students organize information visually.				
14. I understand how to use graphic organizers and verbal tools to reinforce vocabulary development.				
15. I understand how to use graphic organizers and verbal tools to teach students how to compare and contrast information.				
16. I understand how to use graphic organizers and verbal tools to teach students how to sequence information.				
17. I understand how important goal specification is and I have strategies to accomplish this with students.				
18. I understand rules, tactics, and algorithms and when to use them.				
19. I can apply teaching strategies that will assist students in shaping knowledge.				
20. I utilize graphic organizers and verbal tools to assist students in internalizing procedural knowledge.				

Reproducible 5.6. Tools for the Classroom: Putting the Information Into Practice in the Classroom

Teacher Name: _____

Grade Level/Subject: _____

Lesson Title/Topic: _____

Step 1

List a state objective you will be teaching in this lesson.

Step 2

List a declarative objective you will be teaching in this lesson.

Step 3

List a procedural objective you will be teaching in this lesson.

Step 4

Describe which graphic organizer or verbal tool you will use to help students master the objectives listed above.

Step 5

Explain how you will us the graphic organizer or verbal tool in the lesson to be taught. Include a completed sample.

Reproducible 5.7. PMI Chart:
A Tool for Reflecting on the Learning

Directions: Evaluate the session by listing the positive things you have learned in the P (Positive) column. List the questions or negative feelings about the session in the M (Minus) column and any other comments or thoughts about the session in the I (Interesting) column.

P (Positive)	M (Minus)	I (Interesting)

Training Session 6

What Every Teacher Should Know About Classroom Management and Discipline

O ff-task behavior in the classroom costs so much in terms of time on task, not to mention the emotional cost on teachers and other students in the classroom. Most off-task behavior can be prevented through a series of brain-compatible procedures carried out by the classroom teacher. The purpose of the book *What Every Teacher Should Know About Classroom Management and Discipline* is to look at various types of behavior problems in the classroom, possible root causes, and ways to deal with the problems effectively. The material outlined in the book is not intended to provide a quick fix but, rather, meant to guide the classroom teacher as he or she works to help students become aware of and responsible for their own behaviors.

MATERIALS

You will need the following materials for this session:

A copy of *What Every Teacher Should Know About Classroom Management and Discipline* for each participant

Handouts for each participant

Transparencies of all reproducibles and an overhead projector (or other form of digital presentation)

Pens, pencils, markers, and highlighters

Chart paper

Tape, staples, pushpins, clips, or easels to display chart paper

Notepads or reusable notepaper

A CD player and music (recommended)

LEARNING OBJECTIVES

Declarative Objectives

Participants will know the following:

- Which strategies have been used to reach unsuccessful learners
- The terminology related to classroom management and discipline
- The characteristics of learning and off-task behavior
- How to employ teaching strategies to assist off-task learners
- The characteristics of difficult learners
- Teaching strategies to implement to assist difficult learners
- Strategies to use with difficult learners
- The components of a model for classroom management

Procedural Objectives

Participants will be able to do the following:

- Complete a chart of strategies used to reach unsuccessful learners
- Define the terminology related to classroom management and discipline
- Assess their knowledge about classroom management and discipline
- Classify the characteristics of learning and off-task behavior and describe the teaching strategies designed to meet these learners' needs
- Classify the characteristics of difficult learners and describe the teaching strategies designed to meet these learners' needs
- Identify student needs based on a scenario
- Create a campus management strategy based on a scenario
- Develop a model for classroom management
- Implement a model for classroom management

Suggested Activities and Time Frame

Estimated Time: 6 hours

Estimated Time on Task	Objectives	Activities
20 minutes	Declarative Objective—Participants will know • Which strategies have been used to reach unsuccessful learners. Procedural Objective—Participants will be able to • Complete a chart of strategies used to reach unsuccessful learners.	**Activity 1: Preparing for the Learning** Invite the participants to form cooperative learning groups. Refer to Reproducible 0.1. Tell the participants that they will engage in a brainstorming activity to access prior knowledge. Share the rules of brainstorming on Reproducible 0.2. Review the worksheet titled "Johnny" (Reproducible 6.1) with participants. Model how to answer the question and provide an example if necessary. Distribute copies of the "Johnny" reproducible and have each group complete the prompt on the worksheet. When everyone has completed the activity, move to the front of the room and ask the reporters to share the results of the brainstorm. List all responses on chart paper for everyone to see. Introduce the topic of the workshop—*What Every Teacher Should Know About Classroom Management and Discipline.* Share the declarative and procedural objectives for the training. Refer the participants to the book *What Every Teacher Should Know About Classroom Management and Discipline.* Tell them that the activities in this workshop are designed to engage the participants in meaningful dialogue concerning classroom management and discipline.
45 minutes	Declarative Objective—Participants will know • The terminology related to classroom management and discipline.	**Activity 2: Examining the Vocabulary** Review and post the objectives for the activity. Remind the participants of the roles and guidelines for cooperative learning groups (see Reproducible 0.1). Refer participants to the Vocabulary List for Assessment in *What Every Teacher Should Know About Classroom Management and Discipline* (p. xiii).

(Continued)

(Continued)

Estimated Time on Task	Objectives	Activities
	Procedural Objective—Participants will be able to • Define the terminology related to classroom management and discipline.	Instruct participants to provide a definition for each vocabulary word based on what they already know. Have them write their definitions in the column "Your Definition." Divide the vocabulary words equally among the groups. Ask the groups to discuss their assigned words, check the Vocabulary Summary, and review the text of the book to refine their definitions. Have them write the new definitions in the column "Your Revised Definition." Invite the reporters to share their revised definitions with the large group.
15 minutes	Procedural Objective—Participants will be able to • Assess their knowledge about classroom management and discipline.	**Pre-Test** Review and post the objective for the activity. Inform the group that it is important to assess the knowledge they bring to the workshop. At the conclusion of the workshop, they will be able to measure their learning and progress. Refer participants to the Vocabulary Pre-Test section of the book *What Every Teacher Should Know About Classroom Management and Discipline* (beginning on p. xv). Have participants complete the test, and then direct them to the Post-Test Answer Key in the book *What Every Teacher Should Know About Classroom Management and Discipline* (p. 82). Ask participants to grade their tests and record the number of correct answers for future reference.
30–45 minutes	Declarative Objectives—Participants will know • The characteristics of learning and off-task behavior. • How to employ teaching strategies to assist off-task learners. • The characteristics of difficult learners.	**Activity 3: Making Use of the Information From the Book** *Part I—Working With Difficult Students* Review and post the objectives for the activity. Refer the participants to Chapters 1–3 of the book *What Every Teacher Should Know About Classroom Management and Discipline.* Display and model how to create a Classifying Map to classify information using Reproducible 6.2.

Estimated Time on Task	Objectives	Activities
	• How to employ teaching strategies to assist difficult learners.	Give each group a sheet of chart paper. Prompt the groups to create a Classifying Map for one of the topics listed below. You can randomly assign the following topics or allow participants to choose.
	Procedural Objectives— Participants will be able to • Classify the characteristics of learning and off-task behavior and describe the teaching strategies designed to meet these learners. • Classify the characteristics of difficult learners and describe the teaching strategies designed to meet these learners.	*Classifying Map 1*—"Learning and Off-Task Behavior." Have the group write "Learning and Off-Task Behavior" at the top of the map. The four classifications are (a) Self-System, (b) Flow State, (c) Stress, and (d) Strategies for Off-Task Behavior. Then, instruct the group to complete the map with details and information they gathered from the book. *Classifying Map 2*—"Difficult Students." Have the group write "Difficult Students" at the top of the map. The three classifications are (a) Attention Seekers, (b) Power Seekers, and (c) Revenge Seekers. Each of these headings has two supporting ideas—Characteristics and Teaching Strategies. Then, instruct the group to complete the map with details and information they gathered from the book. *Classifying Map 3*—"More About Difficult Students." Have the group write "More About Difficult Students" at the top of the map. The two classifications are (a) Anger and (b) Poverty. Each of these headings has two supporting ideas—Characteristics and Teaching Strategies. Then, instruct the group to complete the map with details and information they gathered from the book. When the maps are completed, encourage the reporters to post the Classifying Maps and share the information with the large group.
30–45 minutes	Declarative Objective— Participants will know • What strategies to use with difficult learners. Procedural Objectives— Participants will be able to	**Activity 3: Making Use of the Information From the Book** *Part II—Effective Campus Management Planning* Review and post the objectives for the activity. Remind the participants of the roles and guidelines for cooperative learning groups (see Reproducible 0.1).

(Continued)

(Continued)

Estimated Time on Task	Objectives	Activities
	• Identify student needs based on a scenario. • Create a campus management strategy based on a scenario.	Create a transparency or handout of Reproducible 6.3, Planning for Campus Management. Participants will read the scenario and review what they learned from Chapters 4 and 5 of the book *What Every Teacher Should Know About Classroom Management and Discipline*. Give each group a sheet of chart paper and direct the recorders to re-create the T-chart from the reproducible. Encourage the groups to discuss the management needs and strategy solutions for Treemont Elementary and write them on the chart paper. When the charts are completed, invite the reporters to post them around the room. Guide participants through a gallery walk to review the responses of every group. (You may want to play music while participants wander through the gallery.) Encourage participants to record any new insights or items of interest they might see. Lead a brief discussion about these revelations at the end of the gallery walk.
35 minutes	Procedural Objective— Participants will be able to • Assess their knowledge about classroom management and discipline.	**Activity 4: Knowledge and Confidence** Review and post the objective for the activity. Tell the participants that they have reviewed the vocabulary, read the book, and actively discussed the topics of classroom management and discipline. Ask them to assess their knowledge and confidence in applying the information they have learned. Make a copy of the Classroom Management and Discipline Survey (Reproducible 6.4) for each participant. Have them complete the survey individually. Then, in their learning groups, encourage participants to discuss the results and create a chart of new knowledge and insights. Invite the reporters to share the lists with the large group.
20 minutes	Declarative Objective— Participants will know • The components of a model for classroom management.	**Activity 5: Practical Application in the Classroom** Review and post the objectives for the activity. Explain to participants that they will create a model for classroom management for use in their own classrooms. Have the participants review Chapter 6 of the book *What Every*

Estimated Time on Task	Objectives	Activities
	Procedural Objectives—Participants will be able to • Develop a model for classroom management. • Implement a model for classroom management.	*Teacher Should Know About Classroom Management and Discipline* and display Reproducible 6.5. Give participants a copy of A Model for Classroom Management (Reproducible 6.5) and instruct them to answer the questions carefully and thoughtfully. Note: If the workshop is being conducted in multiple sessions, you can ask the participants to complete the model at their discretion and implement portions of their work. Encourage participants to record their progress with the plan by keeping a journal, collecting evidence, or videotaping their classrooms. During subsequent sessions, invite participants to share their success and request more guidance. If the workshop is conducted in a one- or two-day session, have participants complete the model during the session and share their ideas within their groups. However, the classroom model should be developed by each participant individually.
45 minutes	Procedural Objective—Participants will be able to • Assess their knowledge about classroom management and discipline.	**Activity 6: Self-Evaluation** Review and post the objective for the activity. Direct participants to share their classroom models (from Activity 5) within their learning groups. Prompt participants to complete the Vocabulary Post-Test beginning on page 77 in the book *What Every Teacher Should Know About Classroom Management and Discipline*. Have participants grade their Post-Tests and record the number of correct responses. Then, ask them to compare the results to the Pre-Test.
45 minutes	Procedural Objective—Participants will be able to • Assess their knowledge about classroom management and discipline.	**Activity 7: Reflection** Review and post the objective for the activity. Review the Revisiting "Johnny" worksheet (Reproducible 6.6) with participants. Model how to answer the question and provide an example if necessary. (You may want to play music while participants complete the activity.) If appropriate, have the participants complete the Facilitator Evaluation Survey (Reproducible 0.3) for the training.

Reproducible 6.1. "Johnny": Analysis of Students Who Are Not Successful

This is "Johnny." He is the child you have never been able to reach. You have tried various techniques and have gone above and beyond in attempting to help him become a successful student.

Directions: In the space below, describe your "Johnny" and the classroom management strategies you have used to help him or her become a successful learner.

_____

_____

_____

_____

_____

Reproducible 6.2. Classifying Map: A Tool to Facilitate Understanding

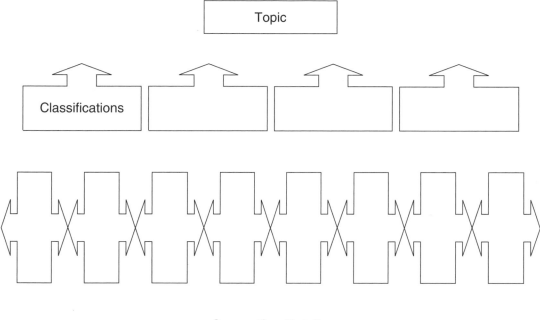

Topic

Classifications

Supporting Details

Reproducible 6.3. Planning for Campus Management: A Tool for Planning on Your Campus

It is now the 7th week of school at Treemont Elementary, a campus that serves students in grades K–5. The school is located on the edge of a large metropolitan area and Treemont students come from a variety of socioeconomic and ethnic backgrounds. While there is a significant number of students who are currently involved in the Gifted and Talented program offered campuswide, standardized testing has shown that over 57% of the student population is performing at least one grade level below expectations in both reading and mathematics. In addition, the campus serves the needs of 32 special education students. Discipline referrals for all grade levels are rising at an alarming rate, but especially for Grades 4 and 5. Speaking out inappropriately in class, an inability to get along with fellow students, and persistent tardiness are the major factors causing discipline referrals. The principal has noticed that the predominant mode of instructional delivery is through lecture.

Directions: Think about the scenario described above and what you have learned from Chapters 4 and 5 of the book *What Every Teacher Should Know About Classroom Management and Discipline*. Then, complete the following chart. Add additional boxes for responses if necessary.

Identified Management Need	Strategy/Solution

Reproducible 6.4. Classroom Management and Discipline Survey: A Tool to Help Educators Determine Their Level of Understanding

Directions: For each topic, place an X in the Knowledge column that demonstrates your level of understanding. Next, rate your Confidence Level regarding each statement.

Learning and Off-Task Behavior	Knowledge			
A. I understand the connection between learning and off-task behavior.	Yes		No	
How confident are you? Rate your level of confidence.	**Rating Scale** (Place a check mark in the appropriate column) Not Confident — Very Confident			
	1	2	3	4
1. I understand intrinsic motivation and how it affects learning.				
2. I understand the self-system and how it affects learning and discipline.				
3. I understand flow state and how it affects learning and discipline.				
4. I understand how the metacognitive system affects learning and discipline.				
5. I understand how stress affects learning and discipline.				
6. I understand the importance of environment to learning and discipline.				
7. I understand the role of the teacher in learning and discipline.				

(Continued)

(Continued)

Difficult Students		*Knowledge*	
B. I understand the differing types of students who are found in my classroom.		Yes	No

How confident are you? **Rate your level of confidence.**	**Rating Scale** **(Place a check mark in** **the appropriate column)** **Not Confident** **Very Confident**			
	1	**2**	**3**	**4**
8. I understand the characteristics of attention-seeking students and can identify them in my classroom.				
9. I understand the characteristics of power-seeking students and can identify them in my classroom.				
10. I understand the characteristics of revenge-seeking students and can identify them in my classroom.				
11. I understand the characteristics of angry students and can identify them in my classroom.				
12. I understand the characteristics of students from poverty and can identify them in my classroom.				
13. I understand the seven primary physical needs that affect behavior.				
14. I understand the three factors involved in any discipline problem.				

Strategies and Difficult Students	Knowledge	
C. I implement strategies that assist difficult students in being successful.	Yes	No

How confident are you? Rate your level of confidence.	Rating Scale (Place a check mark in the appropriate column) Not Confident Very Confident			
	1	2	3	4
15. I implement cooperative learning strategies to assist my difficult students in learning.				
16. I implement strategies in the differing modalities of learning.				
17. I implement the correct sequence of strategies in handling off-task behavior.				
18. I implement strategies that positively affect students from poverty.				
19. I understand how to structure an effective learning environment in order to maximize student success.				
20. I implement strategies that effectively utilize the cognitive, metacognitive, and self-systems of the brain.				

Reproducible 6.5. A Model for Classroom Management: A Tool for Implementing the Learning

Teacher Name: _____

Grade Level/Subject: _____

Level One Implementation: General Behavior Management

1. What will you do to be sure learners feel accepted in your classroom? (List three or more specific ideas.)

2. What will you do to ensure that your classroom reflects comfort for your students? (Lighting, visual effects, sound, room arrangement, etc.)

3. How will you assure order in your classroom? (Rules, procedures, homework, etc.)

4. What will you do to help your students see the value of learning?

5. What will you do to help students set and follow through with personal goals?

6. What structures do you have for placing students into groups?

7. List one strategy that you will try for the seven tools for changing off-task behavior?

(Continued)

(Continued)

Level Two Implementation: Disruptive Behavior

8. What will you do when a student is disruptive?

9. What will you do when a student talks back to you?

10. How will you control your own impulsivity?

11. What is your plan for emergency situations in your classroom?

Reproducible 6.6. Revisiting "Johnny": Reflecting on the Learning

Once again, think about your "Johnny." Using the knowledge you have gained while studiying *What Every Teacher Should Know About Classroom Management and Discipline,* list the changes you would make to help Johnny achieve success.

Training Session 7

What Every Teacher Should Know About Student Assessment

One of the most controversial aspects of teaching and learning is assessment, especially as it relates to high-stakes testing based on state standards. The book *What Every Teacher Should Know About Student Assessment* examines current research on performance assessment, appropriate teacher-made tests, and standardized tests. Standards-based instruction is discussed along with its implications for the classroom. The book also explores monitoring instructional effectiveness and multiple intelligences, and their implications for the classroom. Because we live in a time when government, business, and the general public are calling for educational accountability, we must become more proficient in creating accurate assessments of the learning.

In order to close the gap in achievement for students of color and for English Language Learners, it is important that we provide them with the processes necessary to be successful on high-stakes tests. The "silver bullet" for testing is an important section in *What Every Teacher Should Know About Student Assessment*.

MATERIALS

You will need the following materials for this session:

A copy of *What Every Teacher Should Know About Student Assessment* for each participant

Handouts for each participant

Transparencies of all reproducibles and an overhead projector (or other form of digital presentation)

Pens, pencils, markers, and highlighters

Chart paper

Tape, staples, pushpins, clips, or easels to display chart paper

Notepads or reusable notepaper

A CD player and music (recommended)

LEARNING OBJECTIVES

Declarative Objectives

Participants will know the following:

- The characteristics of various types of student assessment
- The terminology related to student assessment
- How to write classroom goals
- The differing formats for teacher-made tests
- The different types of performance tasks
- The uses for and ways to construct matrices or rubrics
- What constitutes formative and summative assessments
- The different types of objective- and performance-based assessments

Procedural Objectives

Participants will be able to do the following:

- Create a Spiral Brainstorm that details their knowledge of student assessment
- Define the terminology related to student assessment
- Assess their knowledge about student assessment
- List the concept or content to be assessed
- Identify state standards
- Classify state standards according to declarative and procedural information
- Construct declarative and procedural objectives
- Classify formats for teacher-made tests
- Classify different types of performance tasks
- Outline the uses of matrices or rubrics
- Describe the construction of matrices or rubrics
- List formative and summative assessment tasks for a specific objective or state standard
- Create a rubric based on the objectives or state standards
- Design an objective- or performance-based assessment

Suggested Activities and Time Frame

Estimated Time: 6 hours

Estimated Time on Task	Objectives	Activities
20 minutes	Declarative Objective—Participants will know • Information about student assessment. Procedural Objective—Participants will be able to • Create a Spiral Brainstorm that details their knowledge of student assessment.	**Activity 1: Preparing for the Learning** Invite the participants to form cooperative learning groups. Refer to Reproducible 0.1. Display and model how to complete the Spiral Brainstorm (Reproducible 7.1). Give each group a copy of the Spiral Brainstorm handout (Reproducible 7.1). Ask them to brainstorm everything they presently know about student assessment. Instruct the recorders to write the ideas along the lines of the spiral as they spin out from the main topic. Introduce the topic of the workshop—*What Every Teacher Should Know About Student Assessment.* Share the declarative and procedural objectives for the training. Refer the participants to the book *What Every Teacher Should Know About Student Assessment.* Tell them that the activities in this workshop are designed to engage the participants in meaningful dialogue concerning student assessment.
45 minutes	Declarative Objective—Participants will know • The terminology related to student assessment. Procedural Objective—Participants will be able to • Define the terminology related to student assessment.	**Activity 2: Examining the Vocabulary** Review and post the objectives for the activity. Remind the participants of the roles and guidelines for cooperative learning groups (see Reproducible 0.1). Refer participants to the Vocabulary List for Assessment in *What Every Teacher Should Know About Student Assessment* (pp. xiii–xiv).

(Continued)

(Continued)

Estimated Time on Task	Objectives	Activities
		Instruct participants to provide a definition for each vocabulary word based on what they already know. Have them write their definitions in the column "Your Definition."
		Divide the vocabulary words equally among the groups. Ask the groups to discuss their assigned words, check the Vocabulary Summary, and review the text of the book to refine their definitions. Have them write the new definitions in the column "Your Revised Definition."
		Invite the reporters to share their revised definitions with the large group.
15 minutes	Procedural Objective— Participants will be able to • Assess their knowledge about student assessment.	**Pre-Test** Review and post the objective for the activity. Inform the group that it is important to assess the knowledge they bring to the workshop. At the conclusion of the workshop, they will be able to measure their learning and progress. Refer participants to the Vocabulary Pre-Test section of the book *What Every Teacher Should Know About Student Assessment* (beginning on p. xv). Have participants complete the test, and then direct them to the Post-Test Answer Key in the book *What Every Teacher Should Know About Student Assessment* (p. 106). Ask participants to grade their tests and record the number of correct answers for future reference.
30–45 minutes	Declarative Objectives— Participants will know • The two steps of building aligned assessments. • How to write classroom goals.	**Activity 3: Making Use of the Information From the Book** *Part I—High Stakes Testing* Review and post the objectives for the activity. Remind the participants of the roles and guidelines for cooperative learning groups (see Reproducible 0.1).

Estimated Time on Task	Objectives	Activities
	• The procedure for classifying state standards according to declarative and procedural information. • The procedure for writing declarative and procedural objectives. Procedural Objectives—Participants will be able to • List the concept or content to be assessed. • List state standards. • Classify state standards according to declarative and procedural information. • Construct declarative and procedural objectives.	Form cooperative learning groups according to grade level or subject area. For this activity, it is important for participants to work with individuals who teach at the same grade level or in the same subject area. Refer participants to Chapters 1, 7, and 8 of the book *What Every Teacher Should Know About Student Assessment.* Tell the groups that they will be planning and designing an assessment that they can use in their classrooms. Display and model how to complete the Assessment Planning Tool A (Reproducible 7.2). Point out the directions on Reproducible 7.3. Give each grade-level or subject-area group a copy of the Assessment Planning Tool A and the directions (Reproducible 7.2 and Reproducible 7.3). Allow plenty of time for the groups to complete the work. Watch closely and provide guidance and assistance as needed. When all the groups are finished, tell the participants they will have an opportunity to see the work others have done. Ask the reporters to remain at their own tables with their planning tools. Direct the other members of the groups to move as a unit to the table on the right. (You may want to play some lively music while people move around the room.) The reporters will share their planning tools with the visitors for approximately five minutes. Play the music again and direct the participants to move to the next table on the right. Continue in the same manner until everyone has visited all the tables. Host a brief discussion to review any new insight and address any concerns.

(Continued)

(Continued)

Estimated Time on Task	Objectives	Activities
30–45 minutes	Declarative Objectives—Participants will know • The differing formats for teacher-made tests. • The different types of performance tasks. • The uses for and ways to construct matrices or rubrics. Procedural Objectives—Participants will be able to • Classify formats for teacher-made tests. • Classify different types of performance tasks. • Outline the uses of matrices or rubrics. • Describe the construction of matrices or rubrics.	**Activity 3: Making Use of the Information From the Book** *Part II—Planning Assessments* Review and post the objectives for the activity. Remind the participants of the roles and guidelines for cooperative learning groups (see Reproducible 0.1). Tell the participants to refer to Chapters 3, 5, and 6 of the book *What Every Teacher Should Know About Student Assessment*. Display and model how to complete a Classifying Map using Reproducible 7.4. Give each group a sheet of chart paper. Prompt the groups to create a Classifying Map for one of the topics listed below. You can randomly assign the following topics or allow participants to choose. Classifying Map 1—"Formats for Teacher-Make Tests." Have the group write "Formats for Teacher-Made Tests" at the top of the map. Then, instruct the group to complete the map with details and information they gathered from the book. Classifying Map 2—"Performance Tasks." Have the group write "Performance Tasks" at the top of the map. Then, instruct the group to complete the map with details and information they gathered from the book. Classifying Map 3—"Using a Matrix or Rubric." Have the group write "Matrix or Rubric" at the top of the map. Then, instruct the group to complete the map with details and information they gathered from the book. When the maps are completed, encourage the reporters to post the Classifying Maps and share the information with the large group.

Estimated Time on Task	Objectives	Activities
35 minutes	Procedural Objective— Participants will be able to • Assess their knowledge about student assessment.	**Activity 4: Knowledge and Confidence** Review and post the objective for the activity. Tell the participants that they have reviewed the vocabulary, read the book, and actively discussed the topic of student assessment. Ask them to assess their knowledge and confidence in applying the information they have learned. Make a copy of the Student Assessment Survey (Reproducible 7.5) for each participant. Have them complete the survey individually. Then, in their learning groups, encourage participants to discuss the results and create a chart of new knowledge and insights. Invite the reporters to share the lists with the large group.
50 minutes	Declarative Objectives— Participants will know • What constitutes formative and summative assessments. • How to construct a rubric. • The different types of objective and performance-based assessments. Procedural Objectives— Participants will be able to • List formative and summative assessment tasks for a specific objective or state standard. • Create a rubric based the objectives or state standards.	**Activity 5: Practical Application in the Classroom** Review and post the objectives for the activity. Display and model how to complete the Assessment Planning Tool B (Reproducible 7.6). Give each participant a copy of the Assessment Planning Tool B (Reproducible 7.6). Ask them to refer back to the group work on Assessment Planning Tool A. If necessary, have the materials keeper make a photocopy for each group member. Encourage participants to refer back to the book *What Every Teacher Should Know About Student Assessment* to help them complete this activity. Point out Chapter 7 in that book as a source for more guidance. Instruct participants to complete the Assessment Planning Tool B (Reproducible 7.6) individually. Remind them to pay special attention when creating the rubric and assessment. Provide guidance and assistance when needed

(Continued)

(Continued)

Estimated Time on Task	Objectives	Activities
	• Design an objective or performance-based assessment.	Note: If the workshop is being conducted in multiple sessions, you may want to dismiss participants to work on this activity. Encourage participants to record their thoughts about the process in a journal. During subsequent sessions, invite participants to share their planning tools with the group. If the workshop is conducted in a one- or two-day session, have the participants complete the Assessment Planning Tool B within their grade-level or subject-area groups.
45 minutes	Procedural Objective— Participants will be able to • Assess their knowledge about student assessment.	**Activity 6: Self-Evaluation** Review and post the objective for the activity. Direct participants to share their Assessment Planning Tool B (from Activity 5) within their learning groups. Prompt participants to complete the Vocabulary Post-Test beginning on page 101 in the book *What Every Teacher Should Know About Student Assessment*. Have participants grade their Post-Tests and record the number of correct responses. Then, ask them to compare the results to the Pre-Test.
15 minutes	Procedural Objective— Participants will be able to • Assess their knowledge about student assessment.	**Activity 7: Reflection** Review and post the objective for the activity. Display and model how to complete the Ticket Out the Door (Reproducible 7.7). Give each participant a copy of the Ticket Out the Door (Reproducible 7.7). Once they have completed the prompts, invite volunteers to share their thoughts. Or collect the "tickets" and read some responses aloud. If appropriate, have the participants complete the Facilitator Evaluation Survey (Reproducible 0.3) for the training.

Reproducible 7.1. Spiral Brainstorm: A Tool to Facilitate Prior Learning

Directions: Write down your ideas as they spiral out from the topic.

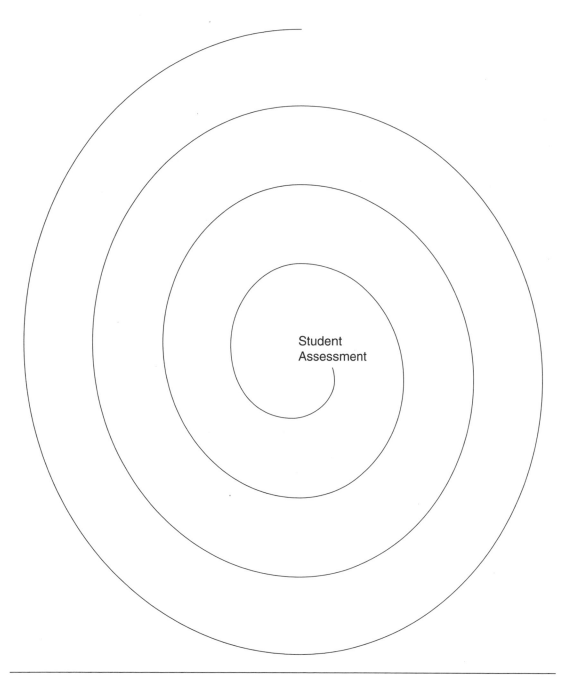

Student Assessment

Reproducible 7.2. Assessment Planning Tool A: Putting the Learning to Personal Use

Step 1A: Classroom Goal(s)

Step 1B: State Standard(s)

Step 2A: Classifying State Standard(s)

Declarative Objective(s) (What students will know)

Procedural Objective(s) (What students will be able to do)

Step 2B: Writing Classroom Objectives

Declarative Objective(s)

1. Students will _____   _____
                    (action verb)   (content/information . . . facts, etc.)

2. Students will _____   _____
                    (action verb)   (content/information . . . facts, etc.)

Procedural Objective(s)

1. Students will _____ _____
                       (action verb)   (content/information . . . facts, etc.)

_____
(product/end result)

2. Students will _____ _____
                       (action verb)   (content/information . . . facts, etc.)

_____
(product/end result)

Reproducible 7.3. Assessment Planning Tool A, Directions

Step 1A

Choose a unit of study that you will be teaching in your classroom. List the title of the concept or content that you will be teaching.

Example: *Introductory unit on Geometry*

Step 1B

Write the state standard that corresponds to your topic.

Example: *Identify critical attributes, including parallel, perpendicular, and congruent parts, of geometric shapes and solids.* (Texas 5.7 A)

Step 2A

Review the state standard and classify the text according to declarative and procedural information. The declarative information is what we want students to know. The procedural information is what we want students to be able to do.

Example, Declarative: *Students will need to know the meaning of parallel, perpendicular, congruent, shapes, and solids. They will also need to know what critical attributes means.*

Example, Procedural: *Students will have to be able to identify critical attributes of parallel, perpendicular, and congruent parts of geometric shapes and solids. State standards do not always list specific products that demonstrate student understanding. At times, the teacher will have to add products. Products that could be used with this objective are nonlinguistic organizers, student-drawn graphics, or a student-constructed 3-D mobile.*

Step 2B

After analyzing the state standard, you are now ready to write declarative and procedural objectives. Note the models on the Assessment Planning Tool. Examples of each follow:

Example, Declarative Objective:

Students will <u>know</u> the <u>meaning of parallel and perpendicular lines</u>.
      (action verb)   (content/information . . . facts, etc.)

Example, Procedural Objective:

Students will <u>compare and contrast</u> the <u>critical attributes of parallel and</u>
           (action verb)   (content/information . . . facts, etc.)

<u>perpendicular lines</u> <u>through the creation of a visual representation.</u>
           (product/end result)

Reproducible 7.4. Classifying Map: A Tool for Teaching Vocabulary

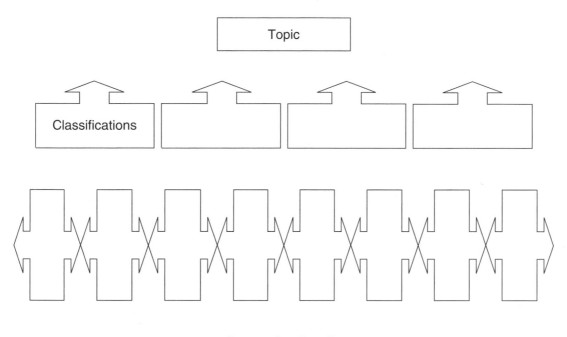

Supporting Details

Reproducible 7.5. Student Assessment Survey: A Tool to Help Educators Determine Their Level of Understanding

Directions: For each topic, place an X in the Knowledge column that demonstrates your level of understanding. Next, rate your Confidence Level regarding each statement.

High-Stakes Testing	*Knowledge*	
A. I understand the impact and importance of high-stakes testing.	Yes	No

How confident are you? Rate your level of confidence.	**Rating Scale (Place a check mark in the appropriate column)**			
	Not Confident			**Very Confident**
	1	**2**	**3**	**4**
1. I understand how to locate information concerning my state's assessment standards.				
2. I understand how to analyze my state's assessment standards.				
3. I understand how to write classroom objectives that are aligned to state standards.				
4. I understand norm-referenced testing and how it impacts my classroom.				
5. I understand criterion-referenced testing and how it impacts my classroom.				
6. I understand how to disaggregate assessment data to determine the strengths and weaknesses of my students and student groups.				
7. I know how to determine the vocabulary that students must learn in order for them to be successful on standardized testing.				
8. I understand how to teach the vocabulary of standardized tests so that my students will achieve maximum success.				

Assessing to Meet the Needs of All Students		*Knowledge*	
B. I understand the importance of assessment as a part of the teaching/learning process in meeting the needs of all students.		Yes	No

How confident are you? Rate your level of confidence.	Rating Scale (Place a check mark in the appropriate column)			
	Not Confident			Very Confident
	1	**2**	**3**	**4**
9. I know how to provide effective practice for students.				
10. I know how to provide effective feedback for students.				
11. I understand the semantic memory system and how to use it effectively in my teaching.				
12. I understand the episodic memory system and how to use it effectively in my teaching.				
13. I understand the procedural memory system and how to use it effectively in my teaching.				
14. I implement strategies to lessen test anxiety.				
15. I understand the differing types of intelligence described by Gardner (1983).				
16. I implement strategies that include the multiple intelligences.				
17. I understand how to utilize Bloom's Taxonomy in the creation of assessments.				

(Continued)

(Continued)

Designing Quality Assessments		Knowledge	
C. I understand how to develop various types of quality assessments.		Yes	No

How confident are you? Rate your level of confidence.	Rating Scale (Place a check mark in the appropriate column) Not Confident Very Confident			
	1	2	3	4
18. I am able to write declarative objectives.				
19. I am able to write procedural objectives.				
20. I understand how to construct objective assessments.				
21. I understand how to create and use effectively the differing types of objective assessments.				
22. I understand how to construct performance tasks.				
23. I understand the various types of performance tasks and how to use them effectively.				
24. I use teacher observation effectively.				
25. I use student self-assessment effectively.				
26. I know how to implement and effectively assess independent and group projects.				
27. I utilize matrices or rubrics in assessing student work.				

Reproducible 7.6. Assessment Planning Tool B: Putting the Learning to Personal Use

Step 3: Monitoring Student Understanding

Describe how you will monitor student understanding for the objective(s) you wrote on Assessment Planning Tool A. List some formative tasks (during the teaching activities) and some summative tasks (end-of-lesson assessment).

Formative	Summative

Step 4: Create a Rubric

A rubric is a written guide of how you will assess student learning and understanding. In the left column, list the criteria that you will use to evaluate student learning. In the right columns, describe how you will know that students meet or exceed the criteria. Refer to Chapter 6 in the book *What Every Teacher Should Know About Student Assessment* for more information and a sample rubric. Create a rubric for the assessment, and then attach it to this page.

Step 5: Preparing Assessment Tools

Decide what type of assessment you will use. Will it be objective or performance based? Create an assessment aligned to the objectives listed on Assessment Planning Tool A, and then attach it to this page.

Reproducible 7.7. Ticket Out the Door:
A Tool for Reflecting on the Learning

I learned that _____

I changed my mind about _____

Because _____

I need more information on _____

Training Session 8

What Every Teacher Should Know About Special Learners

Anyone who studies the history of education knows that where there are education issues, reform cannot be far behind. As educators, we are constantly seeking ways to improve upon our methodology and on the final product—our students. We will not be satisfied until every child is successful. In the book *What Every Teacher Should Know About Special Learners*, you will find ideas for making students more successful in the classroom. All of the teaching and learning practices offered have a strong research base and have the power to make a difference in children's lives. The book discusses differentiation and the brain, categories of at-risk learners, teaching strategies to assist at-risk learners, special education students in the regular classroom, and gifted students in the regular classroom. *What Every Teacher Should Know About Special Learners* is dedicated to providing teachers with tools that will enhance their teaching and ultimately achieve the goal of success for all students.

MATERIALS

You will need the following materials for this session:

A copy of *What Every Teacher Should Know About Special Learners* for each participant

Handouts for each participant

Transparencies of all reproducibles and an overhead projector (or other form of digital presentation)

Pens, pencils, markers, and highlighters

Chart paper

Tape, staples, pushpins, clips, or easels to display chart paper

Notepads or reusable notepaper

A CD player and music (recommended)

LEARNING OBJECTIVES

Declarative Objectives

Participants will know the following:

- The needs of special learners and programs designed to help meet their needs
- The terminology related to special programs
- The connection between current brain research and special needs children
- The categories of at-risk learners
- The programs available for at-risk learners
- The strategies that can assist with at-risk learners
- The laws that govern special education
- The categories of disabilities in special education
- The special education process, including referral, assessment, individual education plan (IEP), and review
- The process of differentiation through content, process, and product

Procedural Objectives

Participants will be able to do the following:

- Define the terminology related to special programs
- Assess their knowledge about special programs within the school
- Categorize the types of at-risk learners that may be found within the school
- Identify the programs available for at-risk learners
- List the strategies that can assist with at-risk learners
- Outline the laws that govern special education
- Identify the categories of disabilities in special education
- Describe the special process that occurs within the school
- Demonstrate an understanding of content, process, and product differentiation
- Analyze a group of students in relation to special needs learners
- Determine the special learner characteristics of a group of students
- Compose a list of strategies to assist a group of students to achieve

Suggested Activities and Time Frame

Estimated Time: 6 hours

Estimated Time on Task	Objectives	Activities
20 minutes	Declarative Objective—Participants will know • About the needs of special learners and programs designed to help meet their needs.	**Activity 1: Preparing for the Learning** Invite the participants to form cooperative learning groups. Refer to Reproducible 0.1. Display and model how to complete a KWL Chart using Reproducible 8.1. Give each participant a copy of the KWL Chart (Reproducible 8.1). Have them complete the K and W columns of the chart. Then, ask them to share within their learning groups. Prompt the recorders to summarize the responses on a sheet of chart paper. Remind the participants to retain their KWL Charts for use at the end of the session. Invite the reporters to summarize the discussion with the large group. Introduce the topic of the workshop—*What Every Teacher Should Know About Special Learners.* Share the declarative and procedural objectives for the training. Refer the participants to the book *What Every Teacher Should Know About Special Learners.* Tell them that the activities in this workshop are designed to engage the participants in meaningful dialogue concerning special learners.
45 minutes	Declarative Objective—Participants will know • The terminology related to special programs. Procedural Objective—Participants will be able to • Define the terminology related to special programs.	**Activity 2: Examining the Vocabulary** Review and post the objectives for the activity. Remind the participants of the roles and guidelines for cooperative learning groups (see Reproducible 0.1). Refer participants to the Vocabulary List for Assessment in *What Every Teacher Should Know About Special Learners* (pp. xiii–xiv). Instruct participants to provide a definition for each vocabulary word based on what they already know. Have them write their definitions in the column "Your Definition."

(Continued)

(Continued)

Estimated Time on Task	Objectives	Activities
		Divide the vocabulary words equally among the groups. Ask the groups to discuss their assigned words, check the Vocabulary Summary, and review the text of the book to refine their definitions. Have them write the new definitions in the column "Your Revised Definition."
		Invite the reporters to share their revised definitions with the large group.
15 minutes	Procedural Objective— Participants will be able to • Assess their knowledge about special programs within the school.	**Pre-Test** Review and post the objective for the activity. Inform the group that it is important to assess the knowledge they bring to the workshop. At the conclusion of the workshop, they will be able to measure their learning and progress. Refer participants to the Vocabulary Pre-Test section of the book *What Every Teacher Should Know About Special Learners* (beginning on p. xv). Have participants complete the test, and then direct them to the Post-Test Answer Key in the book *What Every Teacher Should Know About Special Learners* (p. 100). Ask participants to grade their tests and record the number of correct answers for future reference.
30–45 minutes	Declarative Objectives— Participants will know • The connections between current brain research and special needs children. • The categories of at-risk learners. • The programs available for at-risk learners. • The strategies that can assist with at-risk learners.	**Activity 3: Making Use of the Information From the Book** *Part I—Meeting the Needs of At-Risk Learners* Review and post the objective for the activity. Refer the participants to Chapters 1 and 2 of the book *What Every Teacher Should Know About Special Learners.* Review and model how to create a Classifying Map to classify information using Reproducible 8.2. Give each group a sheet of chart paper. Prompt the groups to create a Classifying Map for one of the topics listed below. You can randomly assign the following topics or allow participants to choose.

Estimated Time on Task	Objectives	Activities
	Procedural Objectives—Participants will be able to • Define the terminology related to special programs. • Categorize the types of at-risk learners that may be found within the school. • Identify the programs available for at-risk learners. • List the strategies that can assist with at-risk learners.	Classifying Map 1—"Differentiation and the Brain." Have the group write "Differentiation and the Brain" at the top of the map. Then, instruct the group to complete the map with details and information about types of learners, brain processing, storing/retrieving information, and the memory systems in their categorization. Classifying Map 2—"Who Is at Risk and What Can We Do About It?" Have the group write "At-Risk Learners" at the top of the map. Then, instruct the group to complete the map with details and information about the categories of at-risk learners, the programs available for at-risk learners, and strategies that can assist with at-risk learners. When the maps are completed, encourage the reporters to post the Classifying Maps and share the information with the large group.
30–45 minutes	Declarative Objectives—Participants will know • The laws that govern special education. • The categories of disabilities in special education. • The special education process, including referral, assessment, individual education plan (IEP), and review. Procedural Objectives—Participants will be able to • Outline the laws that govern special education. • Identify the categories of disabilities in special education.	**Activity 3: Making Use of the Information From the Book** *Part II—Meeting the Needs of Special Education Students in the Regular Classroom* Review and post the objective for the activity. Explain and model how to create a Mind Map using Reproducible 8.3. Give each group a sheet of chart paper. Ask the recorders to recreate the Mind Map on the paper. Instruct the groups to create a Mind Map about a topic from Chapter 3 of the book *What Every Teacher Should Know About Special Learners.* You can randomly assign each group one of the following topics or allow them to choose: Laws that Govern Special Education, Categories of Disabilities, and The Special Education Process When all groups have finished, invite the reporters to post the charts around the room and share their insights with the large group.

(Continued)

Estimated Time on Task	Objectives	Activities
	• Describe the special process that occurs within the school.	
30–45 minutes	Declarative Objective—Participants will know • Differentiation through content, process, and product. Procedural Objective—Participants will be able to • Demonstrate an understanding of content, process, and product differentiation.	**Activity 3: Making Use of the Information From the Book** *Part III—Meeting the Needs of Gifted Students in the Regular Classroom* Review and post the objective for the activity. Have the pilot in each group begin a discussion reviewing the content of Chapter 4 of *What Every Teacher Should Know About Special Learners*. Encourage the pilots to guide the discussion around the key points of the chapter. Instruct the participants to stand in their groups and form a circle facing one another. Tell the pilot in each group to start a sentence, but leave it unfinished (for example, "Gifted students need . . ."). Direct the next participant to add a word or phrase to the sentence. Continue the process around the circle until nothing else can be added. At that point, tell the pilot to begin another sentence and repeat the process. (Adapted from Allen, 2001). Ideas for sentence starters: "Differentiating through content means . . ." "Process is . . ." "SCAMPER is . . ." "Bloom's Taxonomy can be used . . ." "Ways to differentiate through product are . . ." (You may want to post these sentence starters on chart paper, but encourage the pilots to use their own if they can.) Allow several minutes for groups to complete the activity. Then, hold a short debriefing session.
35 minutes	Procedural Objective—Participants will be able to • Assess their knowledge about special programs within the school.	**Activity 4: Knowledge and Confidence** Review and post the objective for the activity. Tell the participants that they have reviewed the vocabulary, read the book, and actively discussed the topic of special learners. Ask them to assess their knowledge and

Estimated Time on Task	Objectives	Activities
		confidence in applying the information they have learned.
		Make a copy of the Special Learners Survey (Reproducible 8.4) for each participant. Have them complete the survey individually. Then, in their learning groups, encourage participants to discuss the results and create a chart of new knowledge and insights. Invite the reporters to share the lists with the large group.
20 minutes	Procedural Objectives— Participants will be able to • Analyze a group of students in relation to special needs learners. • Determine the special learner characteristics of a group of students. • Compose a list of strategies to assist a group of students to achieve.	**Activity 5: Practical Application in the Classroom** Review and post the objective for the activity. Tell the participants that they must translate what they are learning into practice. Display and model how to complete the Student Analysis Chart (Reproducible 8.5). Give each participant a copy of the Student Analysis Chart (Reproducible 8.5). Ask each participant to think about one class of students he or she is currently teaching or a class that he or she previously taught. Once they have selected a class, direct them to determine which students have not performed as well as expected. Show participants how to gather and analyze data and evidence about these students. Then, prompt them to complete the chart. Note: If the workshop is being conducted in multiple sessions, you can ask the participants to complete the analysis at their discretion. Encourage participants to record their reactions to the activity in a journal. During subsequent sessions, invite participants to share their charts and reflections. If the workshop is conducted in a one- or two-day session, have participants complete the analysis individually during the session, and then share their ideas within their groups.
45 minutes	Procedural Objective— Participants will be able to • Assess their knowledge about special programs within the school.	**Activity 6: Self-Evaluation** Review and post the objective for the activity. Direct participants to share their Student Analysis Charts (from Activity 5) within their learning groups. (Caution them not to reveal names or identifying characteristics of students.)

(Continued)

(Continued)

Estimated Time on Task	Objectives	Activities
		Prompt participants to complete the Vocabulary Post-Test beginning on page 95 in the book *What Every Teacher Should Know About Special Learners.* Have participants grade their Post-Tests and record the number of correct responses. Then, ask them to compare the results to the Pre-Test.
45 minutes	Procedural Objective—Participants will be able to • Assess their knowledge about special programs within the school.	**Activity 7: Reflection** Review and post the objective for the activity. Ask participants to retrieve the KWL Chart that they worked on in Activity 1. Have them complete the L column of the chart. Then, ask participants to share within their learning groups. Prompt the recorders to summarize the responses on the chart paper they used in Activity 1. When the groups have completed logging their responses, the reporters should share the group responses with the whole group. If appropriate, have the participants complete the Facilitator Evaluation Survey (Reproducible 0.3) for the training.

Reproducible 8.1. KWL Chart:
A Brainstorming Tool to Determine Prior Learning

Directions: Think about the topics below. Write down everything you *know* about the topics in the K column. Write down anything you *want to know* about the topics in the W column. At the conclusion of the session, write down everything you *learned* about the topics in the L column.

Topics: At-Risk Learners/Programs, Special Education Students/Programs, Gifted Students/Programs

K What I <u>K</u>now	W What I <u>W</u>ant to Know or Solve	L What I <u>L</u>earned

Reproducible 8.2. Classifying Map: A Tool for Organizing the Information

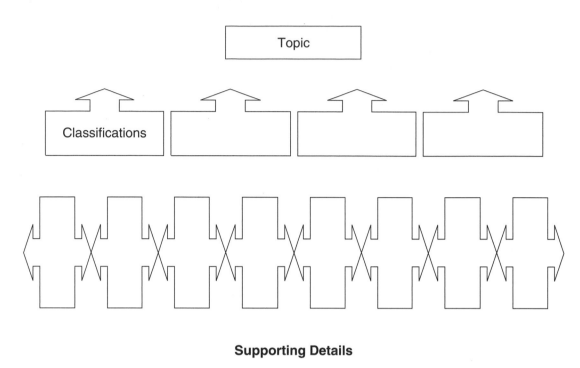

Supporting Details

Reproducible 8.3. Mind Maps: A Tool for Synthesis and Sharing Declarative Information

Mind Maps are often used to help students understand details. The following are some general guidelines for using Mind Maps:

1. The center circle represents the topic or the main idea.

2. The outer circles represent different attributes related to the topic or main idea.

3. Write each attribute in a different color.

4. Each attribute should have words and a visual (symbol or picture) to describe it. Using symbols and different colors helps the brain to store the information in a way that makes it easier to retrieve. Remember, the semantic memory system is not very reliable unless the information has a connector.

5. The descriptive attributes may require further clarification. If necessary, use arrows to connect more circles and show a relationship.

Mind Map on Debates

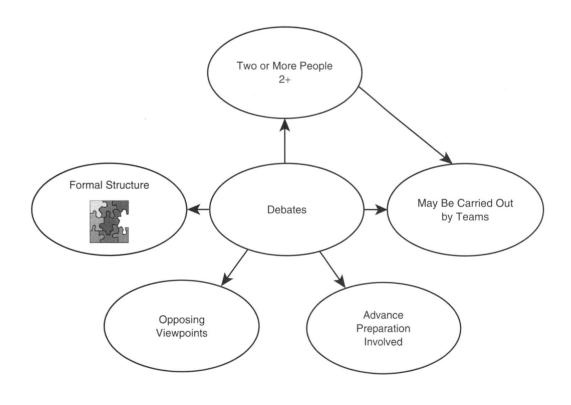

Reproducible 8.4. Special Learners Survey: A Tool to Help Educators Determine Their Level of Understanding

Directions: For each topic, place an X in the Knowledge column that demonstrates your level of understanding. Next, rate your Confidence Level regarding each statement.

Special Learners in the Classroom	*Knowledge*	
A. I know the categories of special learners that can be found in the school.	Yes	No

How confident are you? **Rate your level of confidence.**	**Rating Scale** (Place a check mark in the appropriate column) Not Confident Very Confident			
	1	**2**	**3**	**4**
1. I know which strategies are effective with ADD (Attention Deficit Disorder) students in contrast to ADHD (Attention Deficit With Hyperactivity Disorder) students.				
2. I understand the five kinds of language registers and know when and how to help second-language learners with language registers.				
3. I can analyze student data and assess students who are not achieving in basic skills.				
4. I understand the difference between mental retardation (MR) and learning disability (LD) students.				
5. I can list the characteristics of students who exhibit emotional disturbances.				
6. I know the difference between the acronyms OHI and OI.				
7. I can list the four categories of speech impairment.				
8. I know when a child is considered legally blind.				
9. I know why gifted students can be labeled "at risk."				
10. I know how to analyze data to assess and determine if a student needs to be referred to a gifted program.				

Special Learners in the Classroom	Knowledge		
B. I understand the laws that govern special learners.		Yes	No

How confident are you? Rate your level of confidence.	Rating Scale (Place a check mark in the appropriate column) Not Confident Very Confident			
	1	**2**	**3**	**4**
11. I know the purpose of Title I.				
12. I understand the overall intent of the No Child Left Behind Act.				
13. I understand the purpose of Title I, Part C.				
14. I can state the intent of PL 94-142.				
15. I can describe the components of an individual education plan (IEP).				
16. The concept of "least restrictive environment" (LRE) is familiar to me.				
17. I follow the Family Educational Rights and Privacy Act (FERPA).				
18. I know the intent of Section 504.				
19. I know which student population is affected by the Individuals with Disabilities Education Act (IDEA).				

(Continued)

(Continued)

Effective Teaching Strategies: Graphic Organizers/Verbal Tools	Knowledge	
C. I can list strategies and employ them in assisting special learners.	Yes	No

How confident are you? Rate your level of confidence.	Rating Scale (Place a check mark in the appropriate column) Not Confident Very Confident			
	1	2	3	4
20. I know why context is so important for second-language learners.				
21. I can state which strategies will work for ADD students in contrast with ADHD students.				
22. I know which modality is most often exhibited in students in the classroom.				
23. I can list ways to ensure that tutoring is an effective strategy to use in the classroom.				
24. If I implement computer-assisted instruction, I know the approximate percentile point gain I can expect.				
25. I can employ strategies to activate prior knowledge.				
26. I am familiar with the differences between linguistic and nonlinguistic organizers.				
27. I understand the importance of feedback.				
28. I lead my students to create their own instructional goals.				
29. I can list three categories of differentiation necessary to meet the needs of gifted students.				
30. I understand the importance of goal setting to student learning.				

Reproducible 8.5. Student Analysis:
Putting the Learning Into Practice

Directions: Select a class that you currently teach or one from the recent past. Select several students whom you feel did not achieve the success that you desired. Analyze student assessment data, class records, student work, and other evidence. Using what you have learned from the book *What Every Teacher Should Know About Special Learners*, complete the chart below.

Student Name	Characteristics That Cause Concern	Special Program Available for Assistance	Strategies That Will Assist the Student

Training Session **9**

What Every Teacher Should Know About Media and Technology

The majority of students in any given classroom are either visual or kinesthetic learners; they need to see and experience the learning before it makes sense personally. This is an important point, because individuals learn and remember best those things that make sense to them. If teachers add a variety of media into the classroom, they significantly raise the possibility of reaching all students. The book *What Every Teacher Should Know About Media and Technology* discusses how the use of computers and other media assist students in meeting standards. In addition, the book reviews how media and technology can help teachers provide better, more engaging lessons and assess learning more thoroughly.

MATERIALS

You will need the following materials for this session:

A copy of *What Every Teacher Should Know About Media and Technology* for each participant

Handouts for each participant

Transparencies of all reproducibles and an overhead projector (or other form of digital presentation)

Pens, pencils, markers, and highlighters

Chart paper

Tape, staples, pushpins, clips, or easels to display chart paper

Notepads or reusable notepaper

A CD player and music (recommended)

LEARNING OBJECTIVES

Declarative Objectives

Participants will know the following:

- How media and technology have been used in the classroom
- The terminology related to media and technology in the classroom
- Reasons for using media and technology in the classroom
- Media and technology applications that can be used in the learning process
- The levels of Bloom's Taxonomy
- How to effectively use media and technology in the classroom

Procedural Objectives

Participants will be able to do the following:

- List how media and technology have been used in the classroom
- Outline what they want to learn about using media and technology in the classroom
- Define the terminology related to media and technology in the classroom
- Assess their knowledge about media and technology
- List reasons for using media and technology in the classroom
- Prioritize reasons for using media and technology in the classroom
- List media and technology applications that can be used in the learning process
- Create student products utilizing media and technology for the six levels of Bloom's Taxonomy

Suggested Activities and Time Frame

Estimated Time: 6 hours

Estimated Time on Task	Objectives	Activities
20 minutes	Declarative Objective— Participants will know • How media and technology have been used in the classroom Procedural Objectives— Participants will be able to • List how media and technology have been used in the classroom. • Outline what they want to learn about using media and technology in the classroom.	**Activity 1: Preparing for the Learning** Invite the participants to form cooperative learning groups. Refer to Reproducible 0.1. Tell the participants that they will engage in a brainstorming activity to access prior knowledge. Share the rules of brainstorming on Reproducible 0.2. Give each participant a copy of the KWL Chart (Reproducible 9.1). Have them complete the K and W columns of the chart. Then, ask them to share within their learning groups. Prompt the recorders to summarize the responses on a sheet of chart paper. Remind the participants to retain their KWL Charts for use at the end of the session. Invite the reporters to summarize the discussion with the large group. Introduce the topic of the workshop—*What Every Teacher Should Know About Media and Technology.* Share the declarative and procedural objectives for the training. Refer the participants to the book *What Every Teacher Should Know About Media and Technology.* Tell them that the activities in this workshop are designed to engage the participants in meaningful dialogue concerning the use of media and technology in the classroom.
45 minutes	Declarative Objective— Participants will know • The terminology related to media and technology in the classroom.	**Activity 2: Examining the Vocabulary** Review and post the objectives for the activity. Remind the participants of the roles and guidelines for cooperative learning groups (see Reproducible 0.1). Refer participants to the Vocabulary List for Assessment in *What Every Teacher Should Know About Media and Technology* (p. xii).

(Continued)

(Continued)

Estimated Time on Task	Objectives	Activities
	Procedural Objective— Participants will be able to • Define the terminology related to media and technology in the classroom.	Instruct participants to provide a definition for each vocabulary word based on what they already know. Have them write their definitions in the column "Your Definition." Divide the vocabulary words equally among the groups. Ask the groups to discuss their assigned words, check the Vocabulary Summary, and review the text of the book to refine their definitions. Have them write the new definitions in the column "Your Revised Definition." Invite the reporters to share their revised definitions with the large group.
15 minutes	Procedural Objective— Participants will be able to • Assess their knowledge about media and technology.	**Pre-Test** Review and post the objective for the activity. Inform the group that it is important to assess the knowledge they bring to the workshop. At the conclusion of the workshop, they will be able to measure their learning and progress. Refer participants to the Vocabulary Pre-Test section of the book *What Every Teacher Should Know About Media and Technology* (beginning on p. xiii). Have participants complete the test, and then direct them to the Post-Test Answer Key in the book *What Every Teacher Should Know About Media and Technology* (p. 68). Ask participants to grade their tests and record the number of correct answers for future reference.
30–45 minutes	Declarative Objective— Participants will know • Reasons for using media and technology in the classroom. Procedural Objectives— Participants will be able to	**Activity 3: Making Use of the Information From the Book** *Part I—Media and Technology in the Classroom* Review and post the objectives for the activity. Remind the participants of the roles and guidelines for cooperative learning groups (see Reproducible 0.1).

Estimated Time on Task	Objectives	Activities
	• List reasons for using media and technology in the classroom. • Prioritize reasons for using media and technology in the classroom.	Ask participants to review Chapter 1 of the book *What Every Teacher Should Know About Media and Technology.* Display and model how to complete the Why? handout (Reproducible 9.2). Give each participant a copy of the Why? handout (Reproducible 9.2). Have them write five reasons to include media and technology in the classroom. Show them how to write one reason in each circle. When everyone has completed the task, instruct the recorders to recreate the worksheet on chart paper. Prompt the pilot to lead a group discussion about individual responses and determine the five most common reasons given by the group. Tell the recorders to write those reasons on the chart paper. Invite the reporters to post the chart paper and share their reasons with the large group.
30–45 minutes	Declarative Objective—Participants will know • Media and technology applications that can be used in the learning process. Procedural Objective—Participants will be able to • List media and technology applications that can be used in the learning process.	**Activity 3: Making Use of the Information From the Book** *Part II—Media and Technology in Teaching* Review and post the objectives for the activity. Remind the participants of the roles and guidelines for cooperative learning groups (see Reproducible 0.1). Display and model how to complete the Media and Technology in Teaching sheet (Reproducible 9.3). Give a copy of the Media and Technology in Teaching sheet (Reproducible 9.3) to each learning group. Encourage the groups to discuss what they know about learning processes and media/technology applications. Then, instruct them to complete the worksheet. Have the recorder write the responses on the handout. When finished, invite the reporters to share their responses with the large group.

(Continued)

(Continued)

Estimated Time on Task	Objectives	Activities
35 minutes	Procedural Objective—Participants will be able to • Assess their knowledge related to media and technology.	**Activity 4: Knowledge and Confidence** Review and post the objective for the activity. Tell the participants that they have reviewed the vocabulary, read the book, and actively discussed the topics of media and technology in the classroom. Ask them to assess their knowledge and confidence in applying the information they have learned. Make a copy of the Media and Technology Survey (Reproducible 9.4) for each participant. Have them complete the survey individually. Then, in their learning groups, encourage participants to discuss the results and create a chart of new knowledge and insights. Invite the reporters to share the lists with the large group.
20 minutes	Declarative Objectives—Participants will know • The levels of Bloom's Taxonomy. • How to effectively use media and technology in the classroom. Procedural Objective—Participants will be able to • Create student products utilizing media and technology for the six levels of Bloom's Taxonomy.	**Activity 5: Practical Application in the Classroom** Review and post the objectives for the activity. Tell the participants that they will design six student products that incorporate media and technology on all levels of Bloom's Taxonomy. Display and model how to complete the Student Products sheet (Reproducible 9.5). Give each participant a copy of the Student Products form (Reproducible 9.5). Refer them to Chapter 4 of the book *What Every Teacher Should Know About Media and Technology*. Tell the participants to select a unit from their existing curriculum. Then, ask them to design six student products—using media or technology—to demonstrate each level of Bloom's Taxonomy. Have participants use Reproducible 9.5 to complete the activity. Note: If the workshop is being conducted in multiple sessions, you can ask the participants to complete the worksheet at their discretion and implement the unit plan, if appropriate. Encourage participants to record their progress with the activity by keeping a journal, collecting evidence, or videotaping

Estimated Time on Task	*Objectives*	*Activities*
		their classrooms. During subsequent sessions, invite participants to share their success and request more guidance. If the workshop is conducted in a one- or two-day session, have participants complete the plan during the session and share their ideas within their groups. However, the classroom model should be developed by each participant individually.
45 minutes	Procedural Objective— Participants will be able to • Assess their knowledge about media and technology.	**Activity 6: Self-Evaluation** Review and post the objective for the activity. Direct participants to share their unit plans for media and technology (from Activity 5) within their learning groups. Prompt participants to complete the Vocabulary Post-Test beginning on page 63 in the book *What Every Teacher Should Know About Media and Technology.* Have participants grade their Post-Tests and record the number of correct responses. Then, ask them to compare the results to the Pre-Test.
45 minutes	Procedural Objective— Participants will be able to • Assess their knowledge about media and technology.	**Activity 7: Reflection** Review and post the objective for the activity. Ask participants to retrieve the KWL Chart they worked on in Activity 1. Have them complete the L column of the chart. Then, ask participants to share within their learning groups. Prompt the recorders to summarize the responses on the chart paper they used in Activity 1. When the groups have completed logging their responses, the reporters should share the group responses with the whole group. If appropriate, have the participants complete the Facilitator Evaluation Survey (Reproducible 0.3) for the training.

Reproducible 9.1. KWL Chart:
A Tool for Brainstorming Prior Learning

Directions: Think about the topics below. Write down everything you *know* about the topic in the K column. Write down anything you *want to know* about the topic in the W column. At the conclusion of the session, write down everything you *learned* about the topic in the L column.

Topic: Media and Technology in the Classroom

K What I <u>K</u>now	W What I <u>W</u>ant to Know or Solve	L What I <u>L</u>earned

Reproducible 9.2. Why?:
A Tool for Meaning Making

Directions: List five reasons why you should include media and technology in the classroom.

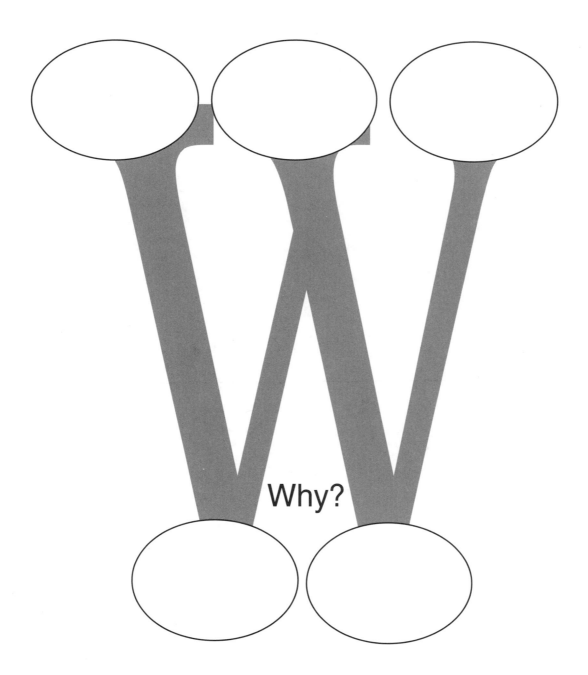

Why?

Reproducible 9.3. Media and Technology in Teaching: A Tool for Organizing the Information

Directions: Review the learning processes given in the chart below. Determine which media/technology application would best enhance that learning process.

Learning Process	Media/Technology Application
Goals for Learning	
Declarative Knowledge	
Constructing Meaning	
Organizing Information	
Storing Information	
Procedural Knowledge	
Constructing Meaning	
Shaping Information	
Internalizing Information	

Reproducible 9.4. Media and Technology Survey: A Tool to Help Educators Determine Their Level of Understanding

Directions: For each topic, place an X in the Knowledge column that demonstrates your level of understanding. Next, rate your Confidence Level regarding each statement.

Importance of Media and Technology	*Knowledge*			
A. I understand the importance of utilizing media and technology in the classroom.	Yes		No	
How confident are you? **Rate your level of confidence.**	**Rating Scale** (Place a check mark in the appropriate column) Not Confident Very Confident			
	1	**2**	**3**	**4**
1. I understand why the use of media and technology leads to brain-friendly learning.				
2. I understand how to use media and technology to reach students with differing learning modalities.				
3. I understand how to use media and technology to motivate students.				
4. I understand how to use media and technology to reduce classroom management and discipline problems.				
5. I understand how to use media and technology to increase higher-order thinking skills.				
6. I understand how to use media and technology to create real-world applications for students.				
7. I understand how to use media and technology to reach students from poverty.				

(Continued)

(Continued)

Media and Technology in Teaching	*Knowledge*	
B. I understand how to use media and technology to enhance my teaching.	Yes	No

How confident are you? **Rate your level of confidence.**	**Rating Scale** **(Place a check mark in the appropriate column)** **Not Confident Very Confident**			
	1	**2**	**3**	**4**
8. I understand how to use media and technology to help students construct meaning.				
9. I understand how to use media and technology to help students organize declarative knowledge.				
10. I understand how to use media and technology to help students store declarative knowledge.				
11. I understand how to use media and technology to help students construct models.				
12. I understand how to use media and technology to help students shape information.				
13. I understand how to use media and technology to help students internalize information.				
14. I understand how to use media and technology in the planning process.				

Enhancing Student Achievement Through Media and Technology	*Knowledge*	
C. I use media and technology to enhance student achievement.	Yes	No

How confident are you? **Rate your level of confidence.**	**Rating Scale** **(Place a check mark in** **the appropriate column)** **Not Confident Very Confident**			
	1	**2**	**3**	**4**
15. I understand the importance of nonlinguistic organizers and use media and technology to assist students in using these organizers.				
16. I utilize media and technology to assist students in understanding similarities and differences.				
17. I use media and technology to help students develop advanced organizers.				
18. I use media and technology to teach vocabulary.				
19. I use media and technology to build connections at the beginning of the lesson.				
20. I use media and technology in the development of student products.				

Reproducible 9.5. Student Products:
A Tool for Meaningful Student Projects

Directions: Select a unit of study from your curriculum. Design six student products that incorporate the use of media and technology to demonstrate the six levels of Bloom's Taxonomy.

Teacher Name: _____

Grade Level/Subject: _____

Unit Topic/Title: _____

1. Knowledge:

2. Comprehension:

3. Application:

4. Analysis:

5. Synthesis:

6. Evaluation:

Training Session 10

What Every Teacher Should Know About the Profession and Politics of Teaching

T his is an exciting time in education. Never before have we had access to so much information about how the brain learns and remembers. Yet never before have we been under a magnifying glass held by the stakeholders in education as we are at this time. If the now famous Coleman Report on the state of education was a cry for reform, it might be said that the current mood and legislation before us is a shout for results.

Teachers are leaving the teaching field in droves, not just because of the low pay, but also because of the lack of discipline, the demands of time and energy, and the politics involved in trying to please so many. Teachers enter the field without being given the hidden agenda for survival. The book *What Every Teacher Should Know About The Profession and Politics of Teaching* is a guide to help new and veteran teachers become successful, life-long educators.

MATERIALS

You will need the following materials for this session:

A copy of *What Every Teacher Should Know About the Profession and Politics of Teaching* for each participant

Handouts for each participant

Transparencies of all reproducibles and an overhead projector (or other form of digital presentation)

Pens, pencils, markers, and highlighters

Chart paper

Tape, staples, pushpins, clips, or easels to display chart paper

Notepads or reusable notepaper

A CD player and music (recommended)

LEARNING OBJECTIVES

Declarative Objectives

Participants will know the following:

- Information about the profession and the politics of teaching
- The terminology related to the profession and politics of teaching
- The expectations for accountability at the local, state, and national levels
- The appropriate use of federal resources
- The facts regarding school choice
- The characteristics of quality teachers and quality teaching
- The characteristics of an effective learning community
- The procedure for preparing, conducting, and following up for a parent-teacher conference

Procedural Objectives

Participants will be able to do the following:

- Generate lists of information about teaching and the politics of teaching
- Define the terminology related to the profession and politics of teaching
- List the expectations for accountability at the local, state, and national levels
- Identify the appropriate use of federal resources
- List the facts regarding school choice
- Compare and contrast effective learning communities to ineffective learning communities
- Assess their knowledge about the profession of politics and teaching
- Plan for a parent-teacher conference
- Conduct a parent-teacher conference
- Reflect on the parent-teacher conference

Suggested Activities and Time Frame

Estimated Time: 6 hours

Estimated Time on Task	Objectives	Activities
20 minutes	Declarative Objective—Participants will know • Information about the profession of teaching and the politics of teaching. Procedural Objective—Participants will be able to • Generate lists of information about teaching and the politics of teaching.	**Activity 1: Preparing for the Learning** Invite the participants to form cooperative learning groups. Refer to Reproducible 0.1. Tell the participants that they will engage in a brainstorming activity to access prior knowledge. Share the rules of brainstorming on Reproducible 0.2. Display and model how to complete the Information Organizer (Reproducible 10.1). Have participants complete the Information Organizer (Reproducible 10.1). Ask participants to describe what they already know about the teaching profession and the politics of teaching. Then, have them read the Table of Contents in the book *What Every Teacher Should Know About the Professions and Politics of Teaching*. Show participants how to make connections between what they know and what they are about to learn. Help them see how their skills will be reinforced and raised to a new level. Introduce the topic of the workshop—*What Every Teacher Should Know About the Profession and Politics of Teaching*. Share the declarative and procedural objectives for the training. Refer the participants to the book *What Every Teacher Should Know About the Profession and Politics of Teaching*. Tell them that the activities in this workshop are designed to engage the participants in meaningful dialogue concerning the profession and politics of teaching.
45 minutes	Declarative Objective—Participants will know • The terminology related to the profession and politics of teaching.	**Activity 2: Examining the Vocabulary** Review and post the objectives for the activity. Remind the participants of the roles and guidelines for cooperative learning groups (see Reproducible 0.1).

(Continued)

(Continued)

Estimated Time on Task	Objectives	Activities
	Procedural Objective—Participants will be able to • Define the terminology related to the profession and politics of teaching.	Refer participants to the Vocabulary List for Assessment in *What Every Teacher Should Know About the Profession and Politics of Teaching* (p. xiii). Instruct participants to provide a definition for each vocabulary word based on what they already know. Have them write their definitions in the column "Your Definition." Divide the vocabulary words equally among the groups. Ask the groups to discuss their assigned words, check the Vocabulary Summary, and review the text of the book to refine their definitions. Have them write the new definitions in the column "Your Revised Definition." Invite the reporters to share their revised definitions with the large group.
15 minutes	Procedural Objective—Participants will be able to • Assess their knowledge about the profession and politics of teaching.	**Pre-Test** Review and post the objective for the activity. Inform the group that it is important to assess the knowledge they bring to the workshop. At the conclusion of the workshop, they will be able to measure their learning and progress. Refer participants to the Vocabulary Pre-Test section of the book *What Every Teacher Should Know About the Profession and Politics of Teaching* (beginning on p. xv). Have participants complete the test, and then direct them to the Post-Test Answer Key in the book *What Every Teacher Should Know About the Profession and Politics of Teaching* (p. 56). Ask participants to grade their tests and record the number of correct answers for future reference.
30–45 minutes	Declarative Objectives—Participants will know • The expectations for accountability at the local, state, and national levels.	**Activity 3: Making Use of the Information From the Book** *Part I—Understanding and Using the Elements of Accountability to Improve Instruction: Heading to the Four Corners*

Estimated Time on Task	Objectives	Activities
	• The appropriate use of federal resources. • The facts regarding school choice. • The characteristics of quality teachers and quality teaching. Procedural Objectives— Participants will be able to • List the expectations for accountability at the local, state, and national levels. • Identify the appropriate use of federal resources. • List the facts regarding school choice. • Describe the characteristics of quality teachers and quality teaching.	Review and post the objectives for the activity. Refer participants to Chapter 1 of *What Every Teacher Should Know About the Profession and Politics of Teaching*. Note: Participants will not form their usual cooperative groups. Have all participants form a large circle around the room. Ask them to number off from 1 to 4, so that you have four groups with approximately the same number of people. Direct all the 1s to one corner of the room, the 2s to another corner of the room, and so on. The four groups should be in opposing corners of the room. Tell each group what their topic will be: *Group 1*—Accountability and Testing *Group 2*—Flexible Use of Federal Resources *Group 3*—School Choice *Group 4*—Quality Teachers and Quality Teaching Within their groups, prompt participants to review Chapter 1 of the book *What Every Teacher Should Know About the Profession and Politics of Teaching* and discuss what they have learned about the assigned topic. Make a copy of the Four Corners Information Chart (Reproducible 10.2) for each group. Instruct someone to recreate the chart on the chart paper. After the groups hold their discussions, tell the recorder to write down the three key learning points and the significant implications in the appropriate places on the chart. Finally, have the groups post their charts on a wall in their respective corners. Show participants how to move, as a group, to each corner of the room. (You may want to play music while people are moving about the room.) At each corner, encourage participants to reflect on the key points and significant implications of the other topics. When everyone has had a chance to review all four corners, host a large group discussion to debrief the results.

(Continued)

(Continued)

Estimated Time on Task	Objectives	Activities
30–45 minutes	Declarative Objective— Participants will know • The characteristics of an effective learning community Procedural Objective— Participants will be able to • Compare and contrast effective learning communities to ineffective learning communities.	**Activity 3: Making Use of the Information From the Book** *Part II—Learning Community* Review and post the objectives for the activity. Remind the participants of the roles and guidelines for cooperative learning groups (see Reproducible 0.1). Refer the participants to Chapter 2 of the book *What Every Teacher Should Know About the Profession and Politics of Teaching.* Display and model how to complete the Similarities/Differences Organizer using Reproducible 10.3. Give each group a copy of the Similarities/Differences Organizer (Reproducible 10.3). You can give them each a transparency if you want them to display it on the overhead projector while sharing. Assign each group one set of the following topics: (a) Effective Learning Community, and (b) Ineffective Learning Community Each recorder is to complete one Similarities/Differences Organizer for the group. At the top of their organizer, have the recorders list the two topics. Next, in the box provided, have them state the similarities. Finally, have them write the differences in the corresponding boxes. When the groups are finished, invite the reporters to present their findings to the large group. Have them report orally or display a transparency on an overhead projector.
35 minutes	Procedural Objective— Participants will be able to • Assess their knowledge about the profession of politics and teaching.	**Activity 4: Knowledge and Confidence** Review and post the objective for the activity. Tell the participants that they have reviewed the vocabulary, read the book, and actively discussed the teaching profession. Ask them to assess their knowledge and confidence in applying the information they have learned.

Estimated Time on Task	Objectives	Activities
		Make a copy of the Profession and Politics of Teaching Survey (Reproducible 10.4) for each participant. Have them complete the survey individually. Then, in their learning groups, encourage participants to discuss the results and create a chart of new knowledge and insights. Invite the reporters to share the lists with the large group.
20 minutes	Declarative Objective—Participants will know • The procedure for preparing, conducting, and following up for a parent-teacher conference. Procedural Objectives—Participants will be able to • Plan for a parent-teacher conference. • Conduct a parent-teacher conference. • Reflect on the parent-teacher conference.	**Activity 5: Practical Application in the Classroom** Review and post the objectives for the activity. Refer the participants to Chapter 3 of the book *What Every Teacher Should Know About the Profession and Politics of Teaching.* Tell the participants that they must translate what they are learning into practice. Prompt them to plan a parent-teacher conference, conduct the conference, and report on their results. Display and model how to complete the Parent-Teacher Conference Planner using Reproducible 10.5. Give each participant a copy of the Parent-Teacher Conference Planner. (It might be helpful to photocopy the pages back-to-back for easy use and storage.) Instruct participants to complete the chart for at least one student and hold a conference with the student's parent(s). Tell the participants to be ready to talk about the results of their conferences at the next session. Note: If the workshop is being conducted in multiple sessions, you can ask the participants to complete the worksheet at their discretion and conduct the conference at their convenience. Encourage participants to record their reflections in a journal. During subsequent sessions, invite participants to share their success and request more guidance. If the workshop is conducted in a one- or two-day session, have participants complete the worksheet during the session. Role-play parent-teacher conferences within the learning groups. Invite people to reflect on the hypothetical conference in which they participated.

(Continued)

(Continued)

Estimated Time on Task	Objectives	Activities
45 minutes	Procedural Objective—Participants will be able to • Assess their knowledge about the profession and politics of teaching.	**Activity 6: Self-Evaluation** Review and post the objective for the activity. Direct participants to share their conference reports (from Activity 5) within their learning groups. Prompt participants to complete the Vocabulary Post-Test beginning on page 51 in the book *What Every Teacher Should Know About the Profession and Politics of Teaching.* Have participants grade their Post-Tests and record the number of correct responses. Then, ask them to compare the results to the Pre-Test.
45 minutes	Procedural Objective—Participants will be able to • Assess their knowledge about the profession and the politics of teaching.	**Activity 7: Reflection** Review and post the objective for the activity. Display and model how to complete the PMI Chart (Reproducible 10.6). Have each participant complete a PMI Chart individually. Then, instruct the groups to complete a group PMI Chart that contains a consensus of the most significant thoughts for each category. When the groups have completed their discussions, ask the reporters to share with the large group. If appropriate, have the participants complete the Facilitator Evaluation Survey (Reproducible 0.3) for the training.

Reproducible 10.1. Information Organizer:
A Tool to Determine Prior Learning

Directions: In the column "Prior Information," write several statements about what you already know about the teaching profession and the politics of teaching. Read the Table of Contents in the book *What Every Teacher Should Know About the Profession and Politics of Teaching*. Under "New Information," list what you expect to learn from the book about the teaching profession and the politics of teaching. In the center column, make connections between the two other columns.

Prior Information	Connections	New Information

Reproducible 10.2. Four Corners Information Chart: An Organizer for Sharing Information

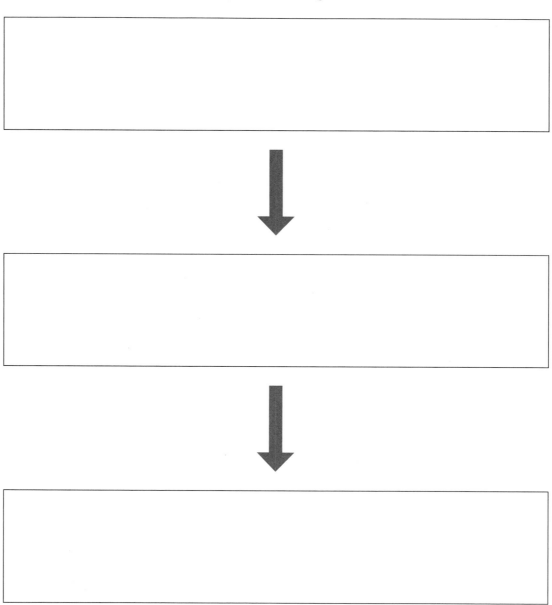

Reproducible 10.3. Similarities/Differences Organizer: An Organizer for Giving Meaning to the Learning

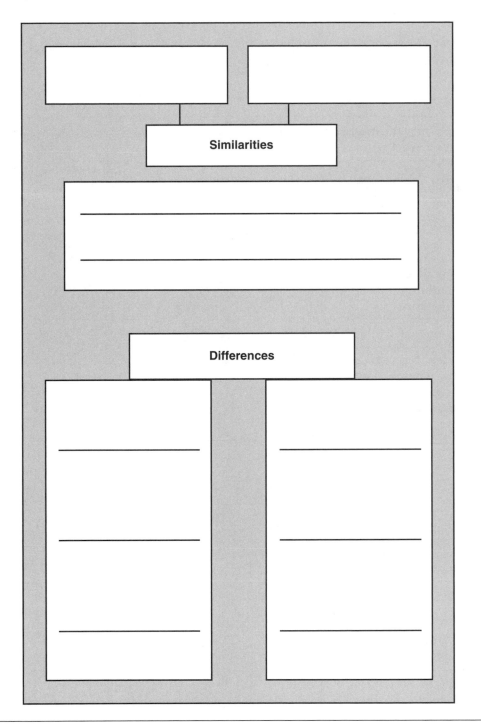

Reproducible 10.4. The Profession and Politics of Teaching Survey: A Tool to Help Educators Determine Their Level of Understanding

Directions: For each topic, place an X in the Knowledge column that demonstrates your level of understanding. Next, rate your Confidence Level regarding each statement.

Accountability	*Knowledge*	
A. I understand the meaning of accountability for classroom teachers.	Yes	No

How confident are you? Rate your level of confidence.	**Rating Scale** (Place a check mark in the appropriate column) Not Confident — Very Confident			
	1	**2**	**3**	**4**
1. I am familiar with my state curriculum standards for accountability.				
2. I am familiar with my state testing standards for accountability.				
3. I know where to locate my state curriculum and assessment standards.				
4. I understand how to disaggregate my school's assessment data and use it in my classroom.				
5. I keep accurate and up-to-date records so that I can back up my grades, notes, discipline records, etc.				
6. I adequately prepare my students for my assessments.				
7. I adequately prepare my students for state and national assessments.				
8. I teach the vocabulary of my assessments.				
9. I teach the vocabulary of state and national assessments.				
10. I understand how the No Child Left Behind Act impacts my classroom.				

Learning Community		Knowledge	
B. I understand that I am a part of multiple learning communities.		Yes	No

How confident are you? Rate your level of confidence.	Rating Scale (Place a check mark in the appropriate column)			
	Not Confident			Very Confident
	1	2	3	4
11. I understand culture and its relationship to a learning community.				
12. I can articulate my school's mission.				
13. I can articulate my school's goals.				
14. I am an active member of my school's learning community.				
15. I can identify the stakeholders of my school and community.				
16. I am an active member of the learning community that extends beyond the walls of my school.				
17. I invite various members of the learning communities of which I am a part to actively participate in classroom activities.				
18. I have identified my beliefs, biases, and expectations in regard to my job so that I may collaboratively work with my team.				
19. I am an active member of my grade level/subject area team.				

(Continued)

(Continued)

Parents and Politics	*Knowledge*	
C. I understand the importance of parents and politics to the success of my school.	Yes	No

How confident are you? Rate your level of confidence.	Rating Scale (Place a check mark in the appropriate column) Not Confident Very Confident			
	1	**2**	**3**	**4**
20. I can articulate the flow of information in the educational system.				
21. I understand the role of the governing body of my school.				
22. I know the role of my state's governing body for schools.				
23. I understand how to assist urban and second-language learners to improve their abilities to function in the world outside the school.				
24. I adhere to my profession's code of ethics.				
25. I conduct myself as a professional.				
26. I maintain effective communication with the parents of my students.				
27. I understand how to plan and conduct an effective parent-teacher conference.				
28. I understand how to conduct the necessary follow-up activities after a parent-teacher conference.				
29. I involve parents in meaningful classroom activities.				
30. I communicate with my principal regarding sensitive issues related to my classroom.				

Reproducible 10.5.
The Parent-Teacher Conference Planner

Meeting With Parent(s) of: _____	
Date of Conference: _____	
Questions to Ask Parent(s):	**Data for the Conference:**
Contact the Student:	**Contact the Principal:**
Room Preparation:	**Refreshments:**
The Conference	
Positive Comments About Student:	**Concerns About Student:**

(Continued)

(Continued)

Things to Remember	
• Relax.	• Avoid education jargon.
• Smile and greet the parent(s) warmly.	• Provide documentation of your concerns.
• Make eye contact.	• State your concerns positively and directly.
• Avoid being defensive.	• Avoid diagnosing the child.
Plan of Action:	**Concluding Positive Statement and Thank-You to Parents:**

After the Conference	
Self-Evaluation of the Conference:	**Things to Remember:**
	• Review your notes.
	• Update the principal.
	• Write a thank-you note to the parent(s).
	• Make contact with the student.

Reproducible 10.6. PMI Chart:
A Tool for Reflecting on the Learning

Directions: Evaluate the session by listing the positive things you have learned in the P (Positive) column. List the questions or negative feelings about the session in the M (Minus) column and any other comments or thoughts about the session in the I (Interesting) column.

P (Positive)	M (Minus)	I (Interesting)

References

Allen, R. (2001). *5-day facilitator training: "Presenting with the brain in mind."* San Diego, CA: Jensen Learning.

Gardner, H. (1983). *Frames of mind: The theory of multiple intelligences.* New York: Basic Books.

Jensen, E. (1997). *Completing the puzzle: The brain-compatible approach to learning* (2nd ed.). Del Mar, CA: Turning Point.

Jensen, E. (1998). *Introduction to brain-compatible learning.* Del Mar, CA: Turning Point.

Marzano, R. J. (1992). *A different kind of classroom: Teaching with dimensions of learning.* Alexandria, VA: Association for Supervision and Curriculum Development.

Marzano, R. J. (1998). *A theory-based meta-analysis of research on instruction.* Aurora, CO: Mid-Continent Regional Educational Laboratory.

Marzano, R. J. (2001). *Designing a new taxonomy of educational objectives.* Thousand Oaks, CA: Corwin.

National Staff Development Council. (2001). *Standards for staff development.* Retrieved June 2, 2004, from www.nsdc.org/standards/index.cfm

Wiggins, G., & McTighe, J. (1998). *Understanding by design.* Alexandria, VA: Association for Supervision and Curriculum Development.

**CORWIN
PRESS**

The Corwin Press logo—a raven striding across an open book—represents the union of courage and learning. Corwin Press is committed to improving education for all learners by publishing books and other professional development resources for those serving the field of K–12 education. By providing practical, hands-on materials, Corwin Press continues to carry out the promise of its motto: **"Helping Educators Do Their Work Better."**